THE Home Owner HANDBOOK OF
PLUMBING
and HEATING

By RICHARD DAY   *Illustrated by* HENRY CLARK

PUBLISHED BY **BOUNTY BOOKS** A DIVISION OF CROWN PUBLISHERS
419 PARK AVENUE SOUTH • NEW YORK, N.Y. 10016

LARRY EISINGER: *President/Editor-in-Chief*

ROBERT BRIGHTMAN: *Editor*   •   JACQUELINE BARNES: *Associate Editor*

L. E. MARSH: *Art Director*   •   JOHN CERVASIO: *Art Editor*

HOWARD KATZ: *Production*

Special Photography by FRED REGAN

ACKNOWLEDGMENTS

We gratefully acknowledge the help of the following firms:

American Standard, Inc.
A. O. Smith Corporation
Better Heating-Cooling Council
The Black and Decker Mfg. Company
Bridgeport Brass Company
Carrollton Manufacturing Company
Cast Iron Soil Pipe Institute
Clow Waste Treatment Division
The Cromaglass Corporation
Culligan, Inc.
Delta Faucet Corporation
Dolve Valve Company
Ford Products Corporation
Genova, Inc.
Hart and Cooley Mfg. Company
Honeywell, Inc.
Johns-Manville
Lennox Industries, Inc.
Mobile International, Inc.

Montgomery Ward, Inc.
National Oil Fuel Manufacturers Association
National Safety Council
National Warm Air Heating and Cooling Assoc.
O'Malley Faucet Repair Company
The Orangeburg Manufacturing Company, Inc.
Peerless Faucet Company
Rheem Manufacturing Company
The Ridge Tool Company
Bituminous Pipe Institute
Sears Roebuck, Inc.
Soil Conservation Service
Stanley Tools
Superior Fireplace Co.
The Toro Company (Moist-o-Matic Sprinklers)
U. S. Department of Agriculture
Watts Regulator Company
Westinghouse Electric Corporation

Created by EISINGER PUBLICATIONS, Inc.
233 Spring Street, New York, N.Y. 10013

CONTENTS

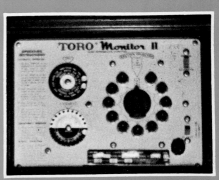

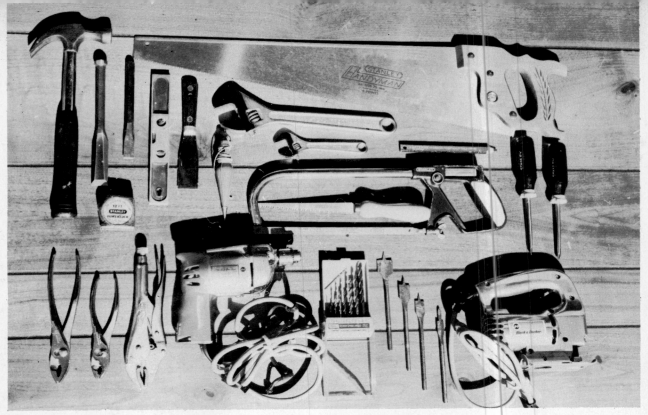

Basic tools for plumbing are mostly the common ones that you probably have around the house: (Top row, l. to r.)—hammer, all-metal wood chisel, cold chisel, measuring tape, level, putty knife, 10" and 6" open-end wrenches, hacksaw, hole saw, pencil, saw, standard and Phillips screwdrivers. (Bottom row)—10" and 6" slip-joint pliers, 10" locking plier wrench, ¼" electric drill and bits, wood-boring bits and jig saw.

Basics of Your Plumbing System

Plumbing problems develop at the most inopportune time. But before you can even attempt to correct a condition you should know how your system works.

TO DO SIMPLE HOME PLUMBING, you need not be a plumber, any more than you have to be a musician to hum a tune. Much home plumbing lends itself to do-it-yourself work and when professionals charge upwards of $12 an hour for their services, you stand to save. Savings of up to 50 per cent are common. Yet, there are some things you should not tackle, so once you know the basics you can determine just what you can—or cannot—do.

When you understand the pipes in your home, you will find it easier to do things with them and to them. Basically, there are three separate areas to study: water supply system, drain-waste-vent system, and fixtures to which these are connected.

The water supply system is easy to tell. It uses small pipes, usually no bigger than 1 inch, and often half that diameter. As you know they bring fresh water under pressure into the house and route it to the various fixtures. They also lead to hose and sprinkler outlets, the water heater and to the water softener, if there is one.

If you are fortunate enough to have a municipal water system, your water supply starts at the street. Leading from the street connection, next in line comes the main shutoff valve. It is a gate valve so, when open, it will not restrict the flow. Closing it involves quite a few turns. After the main shutoff valve comes the water meter which can be located either outside or inside the house, depending upon your climate.

From the meter, the water supply system becomes the cold-water main. Cold-water-only uses, such as outdoor spigots, branch off the main. One branch leads to the water heater and begins a second parallel run called the hot-water main. These mains are usually of ¾-inch pipe.

At each fixture, or group of fixtures, 3/8-inch

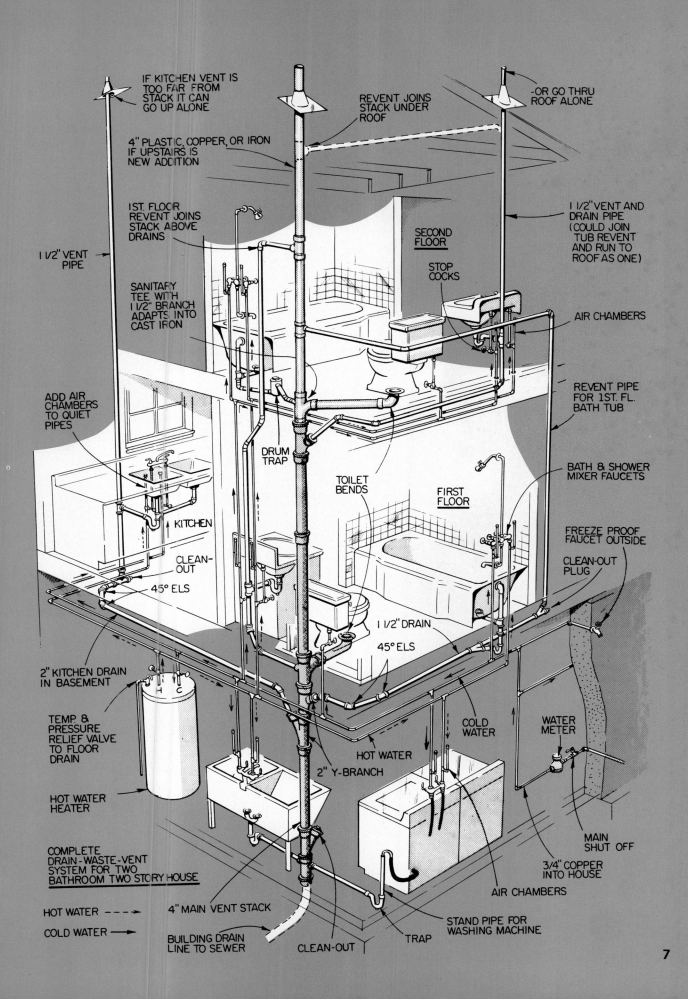

IF KITCHEN VENT IS TOO FAR FROM STACK IT CAN GO UP ALONE

REVENT JOINS STACK UNDER ROOF

-OR GO THRU ROOF ALONE

4" PLASTIC, COPPER, OR IRON IF UPSTAIRS IS NEW ADDITION

1ST. FLOOR REVENT JOINS STACK ABOVE DRAINS

SECOND FLOOR

1 1/2" VENT AND DRAIN PIPE (COULD JOIN TUB REVENT AND RUN TO ROOF AS ONE)

STOP COCKS

1 1/2" VENT PIPE

SANITARY TEE WITH 1 1/2" BRANCH ADAPTS INTO CAST IRON

AIR CHAMBERS

REVENT PIPE FOR 1ST. FL. BATH TUB

ADD AIR CHAMBERS TO QUIET PIPES

DRUM TRAP

BATH & SHOWER MIXER FAUCETS

TOILET BENDS

FIRST FLOOR

KITCHEN

CLEAN-OUT

45° ELS

FREEZE PROOF FAUCET OUTSIDE

CLEAN-OUT PLUG

1 1/2" DRAIN

45° ELS

2" KITCHEN DRAIN IN BASEMENT

COLD WATER

WATER METER

HOT WATER

TEMP. & PRESSURE RELIEF VALVE TO FLOOR DRAIN

2" Y-BRANCH

HOT WATER HEATER

COMPLETE DRAIN-WASTE-VENT SYSTEM FOR TWO BATHROOM TWO STORY HOUSE

MAIN SHUT OFF

3/4" COPPER INTO HOUSE

AIR CHAMBERS

HOT WATER -----

COLD WATER —→

4" MAIN VENT STACK

STAND PIPE FOR WASHING MACHINE

BUILDING DRAIN LINE TO SEWER

CLEAN-OUT

TRAP

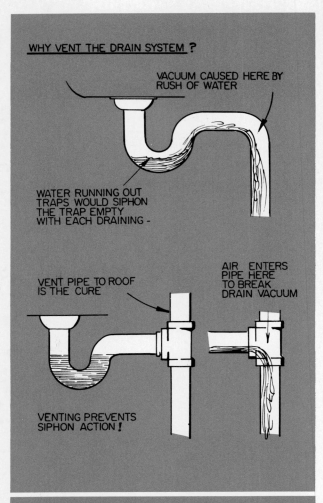

VACUUM CAUSED HERE BY RUSH OF WATER

WATER RUNNING OUT TRAPS WOULD SIPHON THE TRAP EMPTY WITH EACH DRAINING -

VENT PIPE TO ROOF IS THE CURE

AIR ENTERS PIPE HERE TO BREAK DRAIN VACUUM

VENTING PREVENTS SIPHON ACTION !

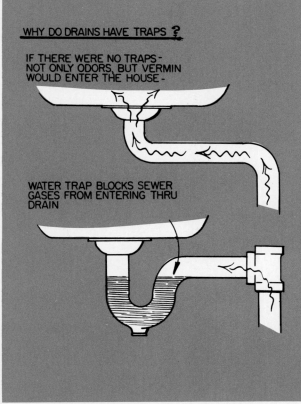

WHY DO DRAINS HAVE TRAPS ?

IF THERE WERE NO TRAPS - NOT ONLY ODORS, BUT VERMIN WOULD ENTER THE HOUSE -

WATER TRAP BLOCKS SEWER GASES FROM ENTERING THRU DRAIN

or ½-inch pipes feed the fixture. Cold water connects to the right side of the fixture, hot to the left side. Except in special cases, a toilet gets cold water only.

Behind the wall at each fixture location (except toilets) are foot-long air-filled vertical pipes called air chambers that trap a column of air to cushion onrushing water when the faucet is turned off. Without an air chamber an abrupt turn-off could create several hundred pounds of pressure within the water-supply system. Called water hammer, this effect has been known to burst a system.

The best plumbing systems station a fixture shutoff valve where the hot and cold pipes come out of the wall or floor. Water then reaches the fixture through a controlled supply pipe.

FIXTURES

The most visible part of the home plumbing system, fixtures, let you use the water, as desired, then drains it away. Sinks, tubs, lavatories, showers combine faucets and a receptacle. The faucets connect to the water supply system, the receptacle connects to the drain-waste-vent system.

Toilets are different from other plumbing fixtures. They use only cold water and while you control the discharge of water, you do not control the incoming supply. That is done by a float valve inside the toilet tank.

DRAIN-WASTE-VENT

The drain-waste-vent (DWV) system carries water away from the fixtures. Between it and each fixture (except a toilet) is a trap. The trap keeps gases, odors, and vermin in the DWV system from gettinng into the house through fixture waste openings. A trap is a water-filled "P", "S", or a drum with its inlet at the bottom and its outlet at the top. Toilets have their own built-in traps, which serve the same purpose.

The pipe leading out of the trap is called its waste arm which leads directly into the first portion of the DWV system, the fixture waste pipe. Usually 1¼ to 2-inch diameter pipe, the fixture waste pipe slopes so that waste water will flow away from the fixture. All parts of the DWV system that are not vertical have a downward slope.

Most waste pipes lead directly into a larger vertical 3- or 4-inch pipe called a vent stack, soil stack, or main stack (if it serves a toilet). Most of those that do not join with other fixture waste pipes, then dump into a vent stack. The vent stack reaches up through the roof where its open top vents into the air. The reason for this is two-fold: to let air in and keep the traps from being siphoned dry by the downrushing waste water, and to let sewer gases out without pressure past the trap seals. Every trap is vented.

Traps that cannot vent into a stack directly have vent pipes that run horizontally to the soil stack and connect to it in the ceiling above the fixture. These are called *revents*. Whether separate vent or revent, the system that costs less is usually used.

Any part of a fixture's waste pipe that also serves as a vent for it or another fixture is called a *wet vent*. Wet vent length is limited by code. The larger the pipe diameter, the longer the wet vent may be and still not siphon the trap seals.

Waste water is collected into one large horizontal pipe called the building drain. This drain eventually flows to the street sewer (if you are fortunate enough to have community sewer system) or your septic tank.

Because of gravity flow and sluggish-flowing nature of household wastes, horizontal DWV

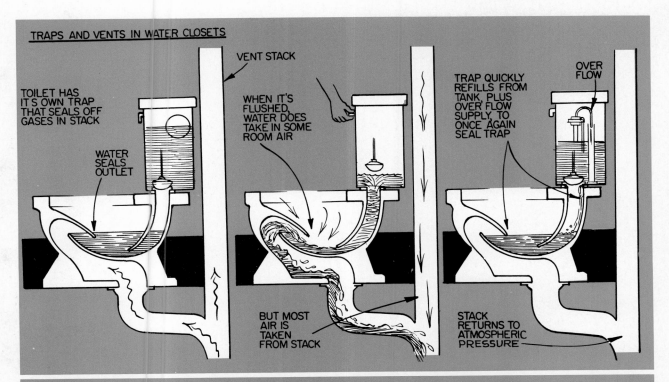

TRAPS AND VENTS IN WATER CLOSETS

VENT STACK

TOILET HAS ITS OWN TRAP THAT SEALS OFF GASES IN STACK

WATER SEALS OUTLET

WHEN IT'S FLUSHED, WATER DOES TAKE IN SOME ROOM AIR

BUT MOST AIR IS TAKEN FROM STACK

OVER FLOW

TRAP QUICKLY REFILLS FROM TANK, PLUS OVER FLOW SUPPLY TO ONCE AGAIN SEAL TRAP

STACK RETURNS TO ATMOSPHERIC PRESSURE

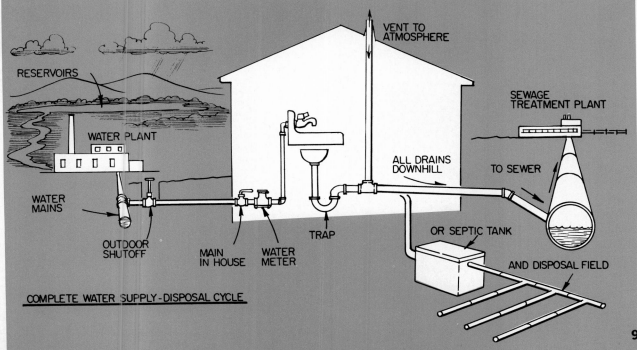

COMPLETE WATER SUPPLY-DISPOSAL CYCLE

RESERVOIRS

WATER PLANT

WATER MAINS

OUTDOOR SHUTOFF

MAIN IN HOUSE

WATER METER

TRAP

VENT TO ATMOSPHERE

ALL DRAINS DOWNHILL

OR SEPTIC TANK

SEWAGE TREATMENT PLANT

TO SEWER

AND DISPOSAL FIELD

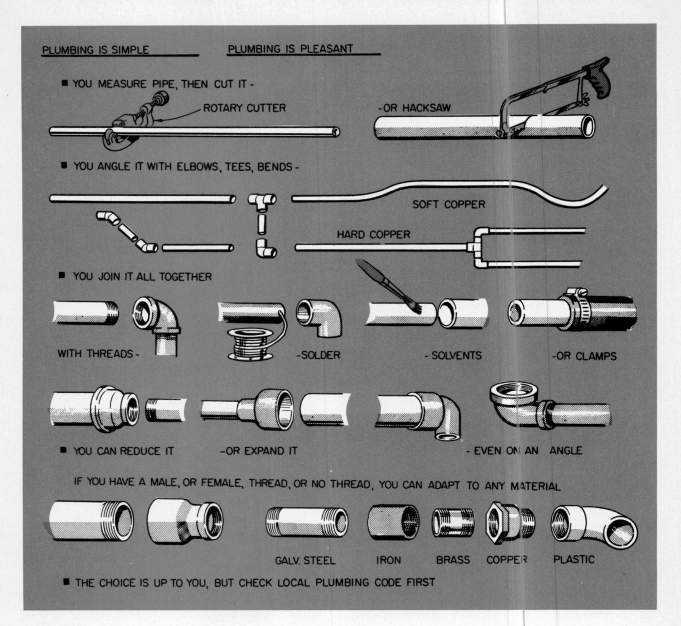

PLUMBING IS SIMPLE   PLUMBING IS PLEASANT

■ YOU MEASURE PIPE, THEN CUT IT -

ROTARY CUTTER

-OR HACKSAW

■ YOU ANGLE IT WITH ELBOWS, TEES, BENDS -

SOFT COPPER

HARD COPPER

■ YOU JOIN IT ALL TOGETHER

WITH THREADS -   -SOLDER   - SOLVENTS   -OR CLAMPS

■ YOU CAN REDUCE IT   -OR EXPAND IT   - EVEN ON AN ANGLE

IF YOU HAVE A MALE, OR FEMALE, THREAD, OR NO THREAD, YOU CAN ADAPT TO ANY MATERIAL

GALV. STEEL   IRON   BRASS   COPPER   PLASTIC

■ THE CHOICE IS UP TO YOU, BUT CHECK LOCAL PLUMBING CODE FIRST

pipes may clog up. For this reason every horizontal drain run should be fitted with a cleanout opening. It is installed in the higher end of the run and has a removable cover for access into the pipe. Some houses have a main trap, located in the house just before the pipe run to the street sewer or septic tank. Every main trap with its cleanout must be accessible in the house, crawlspace, basement or outdoors. Trap arms and fixture waste pipes can be cleaned from the fixture drain, and so they do not need separate cleanouts. In the case of cast iron main traps, the cleanout plug may be brass and, after some years, it will tend to weld itself to the fitting. Unscrewing is impossible so you must cut out the plug with a cold chisel and replace it with a lead or plastic plug that will never freeze up. When you have a clogged line you want to get at the trap in a hurry!

PLUMBING REGULATIONS

Whatever plumbing you install must meet local regulations, called codes, which vary depending where you live. Some can be highly restrictive, even stating that no one but a licensed plumber may install plumbing. Some of the most reasonable codes are based on the National Plumbing Code. Its safety and health-oriented provisions pertain to materials, design, and workmanship.

You must obey your local code or your job may be condemned. The first step is to find out what your code says. You can often get a copy from your city or county building department. If you live in a city, your plumbing comes under its regulations. If you live outside an incorporated area, your work comes under county

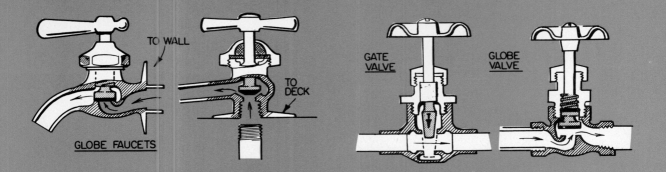

Most of the older faucets and spigots found in houses are the globe-type (left). A round washer closes on a circular seat to shut off the water supply. Even when the faucet is wide open, its flow is somewhat restricted. Same with the globe valve (far right). The gate valve (near right) is usually used for main shut-off valves because when wide open it is the same diameter as the pipe or tubing. Gate valves pass more water.

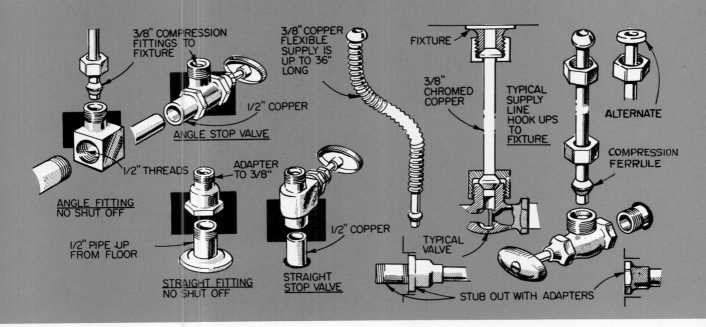

or parish supervision, usually. While you're at it, find out whether the work you plan requires a building permit. Most plumbing does.

Also, find out what inspections of your work are required before it can be finally approved. Most codes call for a pressure-test of new water supply piping and a static-fill test of new DWV piping to make sure there are no leaks.

No plumbing system should contain cross-connections. A cross-connection is any linkage between the house water supply system and water that could possibly be contaminated. If your plumbing is very old, it may have some cross-connections built in. Look for them. A water faucet that discharges below the flood rim of its fixture basin is a cross-connection. Should the fixture bowl back up and fill with water the submerged inlet of the faucet could, under a back-siphonage, draw dirty bowl water

into the fresh-water pipes. A back-siphonage—water being drawn backwards into pipes—can be caused by a drop in water pressure when a fire hydrant down the street is opened for cleaning. Or it can come when a faucet somewhere else in the house is opened wide. The best way to stop the danger from cross-connections is to eliminate them entirely. Any submerged inlet is a cross-connection waiting for backsiphonage. This can even come through a closed faucet. A hose on the laundry tub spigot is a common cross-connection. So is a garden hose used to fill a pool and left submerged in the water. A fertilizer sprayer left connected to a garden hose is deadly in its potential!

To avoid cross-connections, vacuum breaker valves should be installed on all outdoor hose spigots and at the laundry tub if a hose is used there.

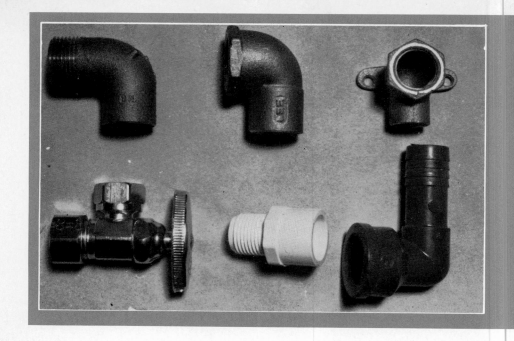

Adapters let you connect from one pipe type to another: (top row) copper sweat elbows to threads; (bottom row) fixture angle-stop, solvent plastic to threads and polyethylene pipe to female.

MATERIALS: # About Pipe and Fittings

Lots of times, doing it easy is knowing what's available to help.

PLUMBING IS PIPE, small pipe for the water-supply system, large pipe for the drain-waste-vent system, and still larger pipe for the sewer.

FITTINGS

Along with each type of pipe comes an array of fittings designed to help you use that pipe. Fittings enable the pipe to branch out, go around turns, connect to different sizes of pipe and connect to other kinds of pipe. Branches are called tees and wyes. Water-supply turns are called 90° *elbows*. DWV turns are called bends—such as ¼ *bends*. Fittings from one size of the same pipe to another are called reducers or bushings. Reducers do the job along a pipe run; bushings do it within another fitting.

Fittings from one kind of pipe to another are called adapters. Adapters are available straight, elbowed and branching out at the same time they adapt. Using elbows, tees, wyes, adapters, and reducers you can make pipe do just about anything you want it to do.

Making pipe even more useful are other fittings. Couplings let you connect one length of pipe to another in a straight line. Unions do the same thing, but let the connection be taken apart easily at any time. Dielectric couplings connect threaded pipes of dissimilar metals, such as copper adapters and galvanized steel

pipe. They are designed to prevent bimetallic action between the two in problem-water areas. A union that does the same thing is available.

Fittings, you will find, come in two styles: standard and drainage. Standard fittings are used for water-supply systems and vent runs in DWV systems. They are simpler and less costly, but have inner shoulders that can trap solids. For that reason, drainage-type fittings must be used in drain-waste runs to provide for smooth flow. Either standard or drainage fittings may be used for vent runs in DWV work.

Specialized fittings handle specific purposes, such as a toilet flange, a fitting that lets a toilet be joined to the DWV system. Those fittings that serve vent runs are used upside down.

"READING" A TEE

When you describe a wye or tee fitting, always state the "run" or "through" sizes first. Then state the branch size. A tee to tap into a ¾-inch pipe and branch off with a ½-inch pipe would be a ¾ x ¾ x ½ tee.

Pipe diameters are only nominal, based mostly on inside diameter. For example, a standard ¾-inch galvanized steel pipe measures somewhat larger than ¾-inches on the inside and a full inch on the outside. If you were to measure only the part you see, you'd call it a 1-inch pipe. So watch pipe sizes. They can fool you.

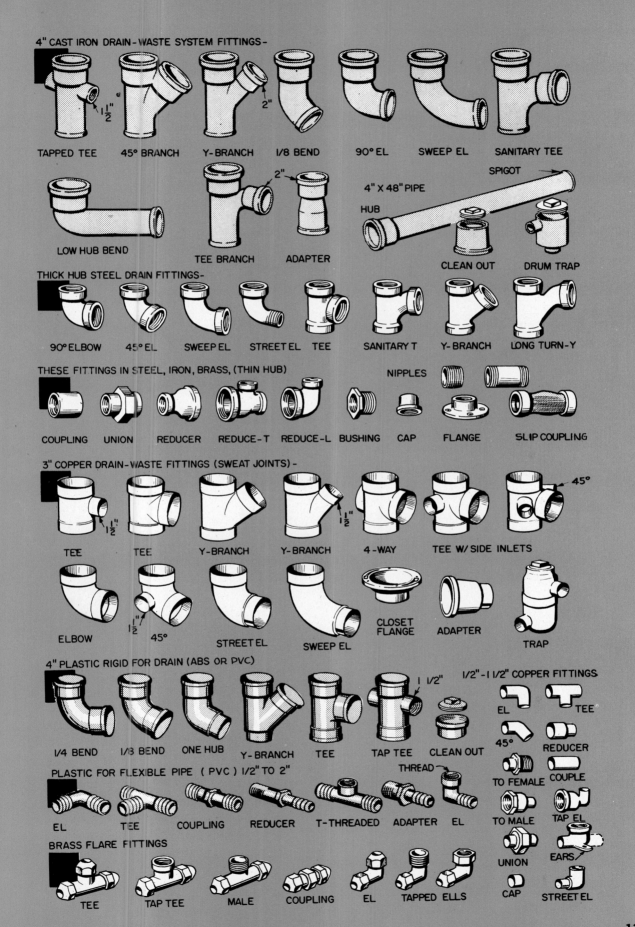

4" CAST IRON DRAIN-WASTE SYSTEM FITTINGS-

TAPPED TEE   45° BRANCH   Y-BRANCH   1/8 BEND   90° EL   SWEEP EL   SANITARY TEE

LOW HUB BEND   TEE BRANCH   ADAPTER

4" X 48" PIPE   SPIGOT   HUB   CLEAN OUT   DRUM TRAP

THICK HUB STEEL DRAIN FITTINGS-

90° ELBOW   45° EL   SWEEP EL   STREET EL   TEE   SANITARY T   Y-BRANCH   LONG TURN-Y

THESE FITTINGS IN STEEL, IRON, BRASS, (THIN HUB)   NIPPLES

COUPLING   UNION   REDUCER   REDUCE-T   REDUCE-L   BUSHING   CAP   FLANGE   SLIP COUPLING

3" COPPER DRAIN-WASTE FITTINGS (SWEAT JOINTS) -

TEE   TEE   Y-BRANCH   Y-BRANCH   4-WAY   TEE W/ SIDE INLETS

ELBOW   45°   STREET EL   SWEEP EL   CLOSET FLANGE   ADAPTER   TRAP

4" PLASTIC RIGID FOR DRAIN (ABS OR PVC)

1/4 BEND   1/8 BEND   ONE HUB   Y-BRANCH   TEE   TAP TEE   CLEAN OUT

1/2"-1 1/2" COPPER FITTINGS

EL   TEE   45°   REDUCER   TO FEMALE   COUPLE

PLASTIC FOR FLEXIBLE PIPE (PVC) 1/2" TO 2"

EL   TEE   COUPLING   REDUCER   T-THREADED   ADAPTER   EL   THREAD   TO MALE   TAP EL

BRASS FLARE FITTINGS

TEE   TAP TEE   MALE   COUPLING   EL   TAPPED ELLS   UNION   EARS   CAP   STREET EL

13

Tools for working with galvanized steel pipe are shown above. Pipe reamer in brace, vise, pipe cutter, strap wrench, pipe wrenches (14″ and 18″), and ratcheting stock-and-die set. The same tools may also be used on other threaded pipes including brass and black iron. A set lasts a lifetime and makes a good investment and has great resale value. If you can't borrow, you can rent sets or individual tools.

MATERIALS:

Galvanized Steel Pipe

Galvanized steel pipe is the most widely used of all pipe. You'll probably get to work with some sooner or later. Here's how.

MORE OLD WATER-SUPPLY systems are around installed using galvanized steel pipe than any other kind. It has steel's high strength and low cost. High pressures and water hammer have less effect on it than on any other pipe. Leakage is rare because the threaded joints between galvanized steel pipe and its fittings tend to seal themselves. Nails driven into framing after the plumbing has been put in cannot penetrate galvanized pipe and fittings. Galvanized pipe tends to form scale or corrode when subjected to some kinds of water. Then, often, the code specifies that some other type of pipe be used.

Because threads must be provided at each joint, galvanized pipe, like other threaded pipes, is tough to install. Cutting threads, even with proper tools, is hard work.

But because galvanized pipe is so widely used, fixtures and all appliances are designed to

be adapted to it. Water heaters come with threaded tappings for direct connections. The same applies to water softeners, many appliances and fixtures.

Galvanized pipe is also available, though not very popular in many parts of the country, for drain-waste-vent systems. For this 1½-, 2- and 3-inch diameters are used along with drainage-type fittings. The large threads are very tough to cut and we do not recommend installing such a system. There are much better DWV materials

Galvanized steel pipe may be used above-ground, but not buried under buildings or embedded in concrete. Outdoor burial is okay if backfill is not cinders. A big disadvantage of galvanized steel or any threaded pipe is that tap-in of new lines is difficult. Anytime you want to cut into the system to add a branch, the mechanics of threading require that a union be installed alongside the fitting to let everything be threaded. Unions are costly fittings. A way out is provided by saddle tees, but these greatly reduce flow. Another way out: For a full flow tee connection you can use a slipnut tee (Dresser tee). This allows teeing off from a galvanized steel pipe run without rethreading the cut-off pipe ends. Slip couplings rather than threads are used.

NIPPLES AVAILABLE

The tools for working with galvanized steel (as well as threaded brass) pipe are the costliest of any. On small jobs you can do without buying them, by using ready-made short lengths of pipes called nipples. Nipples are threaded on both ends. A "close" nipple is the shortest, containing threads along its entire length. A "short" nipple is a little longer, leaving a small gap between fittings. Other nipples are made 1½, 2, 2½, 3, 4, 6, 8, 10, and 12 inches long, end to end. Some dealers carry 2-, 3- and 4-foot nipples, ready made.

Pipe threads are called *male* or outside threads. Fitting threads are called *female* or inside threads. Don't ask why.

Galvanized pipes are available in 21-foot lengths and diameters of 3/8, ½, ¾, 1-inch and larger and smaller. These always refer to nominal inside diameter. Outside diameter measures about ¼ inch more, allowing for wall thickness. Full lengths are threaded on both ends and come with one coupling loosely screwed on.

Three sizes of galvanized steel pipe: 3/8", ½", and ¾". All have threaded ends to connect to threaded galvanized-steel fittings. A wide range of sizes are available. Note how threads taper.

Slip-coupling with rubber O-ring seals at each end lets you fasten two galvanized steel pipes together without the need for threading the ends of the pipe or using a union. A great labor saver.

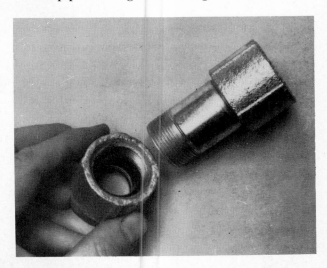

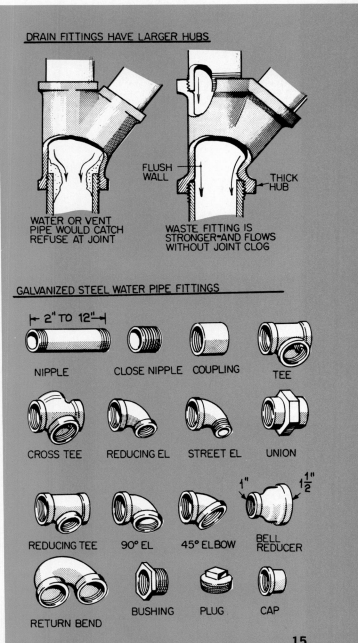

DRAIN FITTINGS HAVE LARGER HUBS

FLUSH WALL

THICK HUB

WATER OR VENT PIPE WOULD CATCH REFUSE AT JOINT

WASTE FITTING IS STRONGER—AND FLOWS WITHOUT JOINT CLOG

GALVANIZED STEEL WATER PIPE FITTINGS

2" TO 12"

NIPPLE CLOSE NIPPLE COUPLING TEE

CROSS TEE REDUCING EL STREET EL UNION

REDUCING TEE 90° EL 45° ELBOW BELL REDUCER

RETURN BEND BUSHING PLUG CAP

These are the three popular sizes you will find in a home. The ½" line (left) serves the hot water heater or range. The ¾" line (center) feeds the furnace. Main lines are usually 1".

Note that this regular galvanized ¾" T fitting at the left is identical to the black iron T. The working techniques of both pipe are the same; you need plenty of muscle and cutting oil.

This is the typical bronze gas valve you have in your home if, of course, you use gas. Each appliance should have a separate valve, clearly labeled. A quarter turn shuts off the supply.

Black Iron Pipe

Unless you run your own gas lines, you will probably never use black iron pipe. It is cheaper than galvanized but just as tough to handle.

BLACK IRON PIPE is used primarily for gas piping. Galvanized pipe is usually not permitted for piping gas because flakes of the galvanizing can drop off into the gas stream and find their way to small burner orifices where they may put out the burner flame and, if safety cutoff devices fail, let gas escape into the house.

Black iron pipe comes in the same sizes as galvanized pipe and the fittings are interchangeable. But don't mix them, because you can be made to tear out a whole run of black pipe to remove one galvanized fitting and replace it with a black one!

SIZE IS DIFFERENT

Choosing pipe sizes for gas runs is not as simple as for water-supply piping. The smallest gas pipe permitted in a system is usually ½-inch, where it supplies only a stove or a water heater. The pipe size coming from the gas meter is determined by how many and what size appliances must be served. Figuring this is a job for your gas utility. Ask them to help plan. They'll need to know the BTU (British Thermal Unit) input rating of each gas appliance along with the distance the appliance is located from your meter. If any extra-long piping runs are required, or you have too many gas appliances, you may find you should not attempt to add another gas eater. Such may be the case with a swimming pool heater or an outdoor barbecue. Incidentally, pipe sizes for natural gas are larger than for more concentrated LP gas.

Once you have determined exactly what is required, you should be able to make the pipe installation yourself. Black pipe to be buried should be the coated kind; otherwise it has no protection against corrosion. The coating may be a factory-applied vinyl covering or a factory finish. Joints and openings in this coating should be wrapped with plastic tape.

Threaded Brass Pipe

In areas where the building code outlaws lead solder and copper tubing, brass pipe is widely used. It is expensive but will outlast any home.

That gleam you see is not gold but you might think it is after purchasing a 20′ length. The 3/8″ feed lavatories and toilets; the ½″ kitchen sinks and water heaters. Main branch is ¾″.

WHERE WATER IS CORROSIVE to galvanized steel or tends to build up scale, threaded brass pipe is used. It may even be a code requirement. Brass pipe is expensive compared to other pipe types. If your house has it, it has the finest water supply system going. Brass has the strength benefits of galvanized steel. Nails won't puncture it; high pressure won't harm it. Unlike steel, its inner walls are so smooth they present little resistance to water flow. About the only damage it suffers is when connected to galvanized steel pipe without a dielectric coupling or union in a corrosive-water area. If you extend a brass water system with galvanized steel, you should use such a connector between the two kinds of pipe. Copper and plastic extensions from a brass system require no special protection, for they do not create harmful bimetallic action with brass.

Like galvanized steel, brass has threaded fitting drawbacks because costly threading tools are necessary. However, one advantage brass has over galvanized threaded pipe is that when threads are cut, a protective oxide coating quickly forms again.

STRAP WRENCH

Brass, being the Rolls Royce of pipes, calls for extra care in pipe assembly. Whereas on steel pipe you would screw the joints together with serrated-jaw pipe wrenches and think nothing of it, the use of these tools mars the fine appearance of brass pipe. For a workmanlike job it should be tightened with a strap wrench, so as not to deface the surface.

VALVES

Most valves are made of brass. They may be installed in a run of galvanized steel pipe without dielectric fittings, provided the water is not highly corrosive and a good joint material is used on the pipe threads. More on that later.

Compared to steel, brass is soft so some pros use a strap wrench on the pipe and a regular wrench on the fittings. If you will accept a few nicks and burrs you can use regular pipe wrench.

COPPER TUBING: Two basic kinds: rigid, hard-temper tubing is usually used in exposed locations where a straight runs and elbow turns look good. It takes soldered joints only. Coiled soft-temper flexible copper tubing is most often used in remodeling work because the flexible lengths are easily threaded through walls, fewer fittings are required. It takes the regular soldered, flare or compression fittings.

MATERIALS: Copper Tubing/Pipe

Copper tubing and pipe has long been a favorite in plumbing, heating and cooling. It works easily and will last many lifetimes.

COPPER IS THE MOST versatile pipe for plumbing. It is reasonably easy to install, resists corrosion and scale build-up, and serves both water-supply and drain-waste-vent systems. While sweat-type solder fittings are most commonly used, copper pipe may be joined with flare and compression fittings if desired. Copper pipe is light in weight compared to like-sized steel pipe. Its sweated joints can be made with everyday shop tools. Copper builds what's considered a permanent plumbing system. The material resists corrosion and scale build-up. Additions to a copper system are simple by sawing through the pipe and installing a tee or whatever style of branch is needed.

Copper pipe can be punctured when nailing wall materials so care should be taken to protect pipes from such damage. Straps installed wherever copper pipes pass through wood framing members will prevent nailing in those locations. Of course, copper costs more than steel or plastic pipe but less than brass. A minor copper disadvantage of which you should be aware is the fire danger when using a flame to solder the joints.

HARD VS. SOFT

Copper pipe comes in two types: hard-temper and soft-temper. Hard-temper pipe is straight, rigid, while soft-temper is flexible, bendable. The smooth bends of a copper system

made with soft-temper copper water tubing present very little resistance to flow. Moreover, it's easier to thread into walls in remodeling work. Usually a pipe one size smaller than for galvanized steel pipe will provide a good rate of flow. Copper water pipe (or tubing) is designated by nominal sizes with the outside diameter always 1/8-inch larger than the nominal size. Inside diameters are close to but not always equal to the nominal size. Air-conditioning/refrigeration tubing goes by outside diameter. Wall thickness of copper tubing can vary without changing the outside diameter. You can get copper tubing in three wall thicknesses: Type K, which has thick walls; Type L, which is the most commonly used wall thickness for home plumbing; and Type M, which is low-cost, thin-wall tubing. All fit the same sweat-type fittings but because the outside diameter is the same in each, Type K tubing is slightly smaller in inside diameter than Types L and M.

When buying copper pipe (or tubing) you can get into a lot of trouble over the size question. You may end up with a fitting too large or a pipe too small. For this reason you're safest to spell it out: "I want 60 feet of ½-inch Type L flexible copper water tubing ½-inch inside diameter." For fittings say, "I want four 90° copper sweat elbows for ½-inch *ID* tubing. You will eliminate mistakes by being specific.

Types K, L, and M copper tube are available

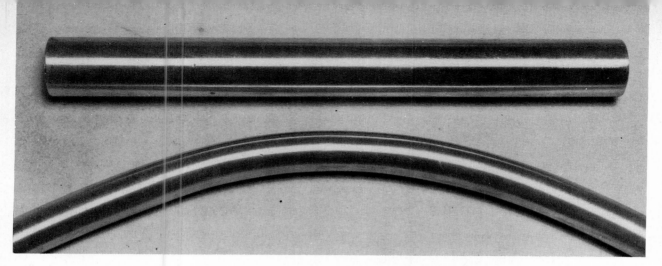

Every home will use hard-temper (above) and soft. Straight lengths of hard tubing are preferred because they make a more workmanlike job. Soft-temper tubing is always used for the water supply from your main or well (unless plastic is used). If the supply line must be joined underground, flare fittings are used.

Three sizes of copper water tubing most often used in home plumbing are (left to right) 3/8", 1/2" and 3/4". Copper's smooth inner walls deliver more water than comparable sizes of galvanized steel pipe, less than plastic pipe.

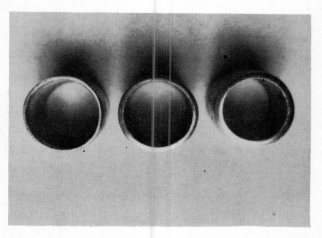

Copper tubing comes in three wall thickness for a variety of uses. Thinnest type M (left) serves most needs (see text). Type L (center) is most popular. Thickest type K, is rarely used.

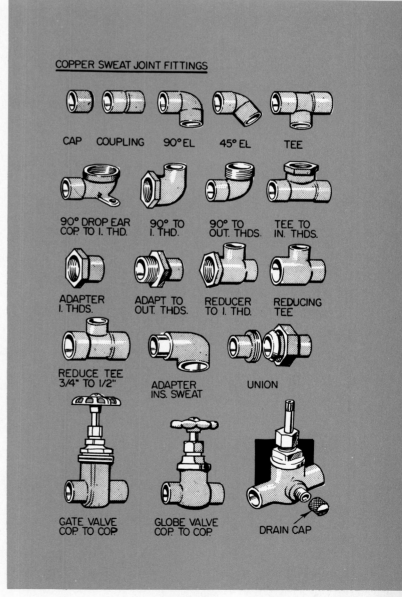

COPPER SWEAT JOINT FITTINGS

CAP COUPLING 90° EL 45° EL TEE

90° DROP EAR COP. TO I. THD. 90° TO I. THD. 90° TO OUT. THDS. TEE TO IN. THDS.

ADAPTER I. THDS. ADAPT TO OUT. THDS. REDUCER TO I. THD. REDUCING TEE

REDUCE TEE 3/4" TO 1/2" ADAPTER INS. SWEAT UNION

GATE VALVE COP. TO COP. GLOBE VALVE COP. TO COP. DRAIN CAP in hard-temper straight lengths, 20 feet long. Also, Types K and L may be had in soft-temper flexible tubing, usually 30 or 60 feet long. You can often get cut-to-length copper tubing from a dealer by paying a somewhat higher price per foot for exactly the length you need. Hard-temper tubing may be joined only by sweat-soldering or annealing the end and using a flare fitting. Soft-temper tubing may be joined with solder, flare or compression fittings.

FOR DRAINS

Copper drainage pipe (DWV) is thinner-walled than similar sizes of water pipe and is not generally used under pressure, though it can be. Its outside diameter is always 1/8 inch larger than its nominal inside measurement, by which it is designated. Copper drainage tube is joined with DWV drainage-type fittings. These are sweat-soldered to pipe ends. When used for water under pressure, pressure-type fittings should be used. Diameters of 1½-, 2-, and 3-inches are normally used in DWV work. Pipe lengths are 20 feet.

While Type L copper water pipe will withstand working pressures of 600 psi, the sweat-soldered joints you make will take only about 100 psi. Thus, the joints are the weak links in a copper water-supply system. Water hammer can blow joints apart so supply pipes should be fitted with air chambers. For this same reason, sweat-soldered copper tubing is not used for gas lines, although some codes permit flare and compression fittings for gas service, especially LP gas. Such a system properly made up will withstand pressures of 700 psi, the same as one made of black iron pipe.

Soft-temper copper pipe or tubing has the advantage that in it water can freeze several times without bursting the pipe. But remember, with each freeze the diameter gets larger—and the walls get thinner! With the hard-temper tubes and with steel pipe the first freezing cracks the pipe.

Pipe Type Recommendations

Here are the most sensible recommendations I've seen:

For house water supply piping use Type M tubing, both above and below ground where straight runs and fittings are wanted. Or use soft-temper Type L tubing where you wish to bend the pipes and eliminate some fittings. For hot-water heating systems use Type L flexible for most uses and Type M where straight lengths with fittings are wanted. Color-coding of tubing is as follows:

Green—Type K
Blue—Type L
Red—Type M
Yellow—Copper drainage
Crimson—Refrigeration

(appears on cartons only).

COPPER PRESSURE FITTINGS

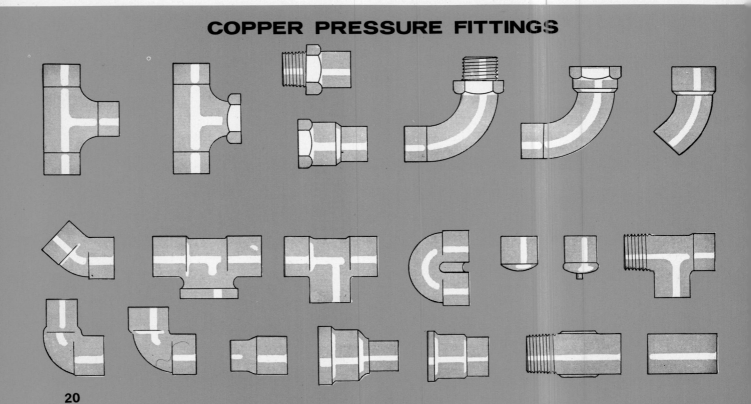

20

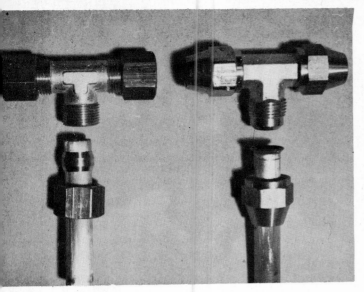

Joining copper tubing without solder, you have two choices: compression fittings (left) and flare fittings. Compression one uses nuts and brass ferrules; flare uses nuts, flared ends. Both are good.

Tubing cutters make neat, clean square cuts in copper piping without squashing the ends out of round. Standard cutter (left) is easiest to work; close quarter cutter works well in tight spaces.

COPPER DRAINAGE WASTE VENT FITTINGS

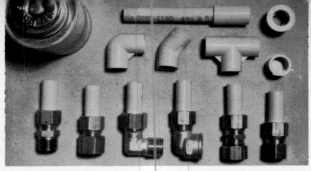

CPVC fittings (left to right): (top row) Solvent, pipe with coupling, bushing; (center row)—90° elbow, 45° elbow, tee, cap; (bottom row). Various adapters. CPVC cost substantially more than PVC.

Adapters for plastic pipes to threaded pipe fittings should not be used with ordinary pipe dope, because the dope may soften the plastic. Instead, use a plastic thread dope made for the purpose.

MATERIALS:

Plastic Water Supply Pipe

Plastic pipe is do-it-yourself pipe. If your code is modern enough to let you use it, you'll like working with plastic pipe.

THE EASIEST-TO-USE PIPE for do-it-yourself water-supply installation is plastic. Like copper, it comes in sizes and fittings for both water-supply and drain-waste-vent use. There are also two other kinds of plastic pipe for cold-water-only use.

If there are no old-fashioned codes preventing it, we recommend the use of plastic piping. Besides being easy to cut and join, it is low in cost. It's lightweight, too. The inner walls of plastic pipe are so smooth that water passes easily through. A smaller size can do the same job as a size larger metal pipe. Normally, though, the same size is used.

For cold and hot-water lines, plastic pipe is naturally insulating and eliminates sweating in cold-water lines. For hot-water lines, the plastic cuts heat loss, which can be considerable with metal piping. Plastic pipes may be installed above or below ground.

Drawbacks are few. Only one type of plastic pipe may be used with hot water: CPVC. The others are intended for cold-water lines only. Plastic pipe is easily punctured by nailing and so must be protected the same as with copper tubing. Over-temperatures and over-pressures must be avoided. With any other kind of pipe, a misjudged fitting, once assembled, can be taken apart and refitted. Not so with solvent-welded joints. If you make a mistake, you have to saw the fitting out of the run and install a new one with suitable couplings to join it to the cut-off ends. To be sure everything fits correctly the first time, thought must be given before making up each joint. Otherwise, the useless pile of sawed-out parts left over after a job can cancel out any savings in material or time over some other type of pipe.

CPVC PLASTIC

For water-supply systems, the pipe to use is CPVC (Chlorinated PolyVinyl Chloride). The trouble with most plastic pipes is that they soften when hot. CPVC does only slightly as it is chemically toughened against heat by putting an extra chlorine atom into the composition. CPVC pipe is rated to withstand 100 psi (pounds per square inch) at 180° F.).

CPVC pipe is widely available, even through mail order. Genova, Inc., the pioneer in producing CPVC pipe, standardized on two sizes, ¾- and ½-inch in smaller copper-pipe sizes. The others have followed suit. The Genova people theorized sensibly that 3/8-inch pipe is so little used in home plumbing systems that it may as well be eliminated entirely. Having only two sizes makes ordering that much easier.

CPVC pipe comes in 10-foot lengths. Genova offers its pipe in two colors, orange and green, representing hot-and-cold water lines. Such a system could be color-coded throughout the house. Either color may be used for all pipes, hot or cold.

Fittings for CPVC are not as extensive as those for galvanized steel pipe, but they are sufficient to do the job. Use CPVC solvent for joining; it takes a quarter pint to do 63 ½-inch joints. The Genova system uses two chemicals: a cleaner and a solvent.

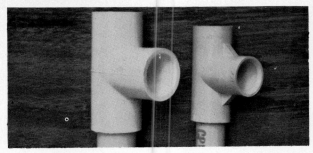

Both fittings shown above are ½″ size, PVC on the left, CPVC On the right. The larger PVC pipe is based on steel pipe sizes, while the smaller CPVC is based on regular copper tubing sizes.

COLD WATER ONLY

CPVC pipe's lower-temperature cousin, PVC pipe (PolyVinyl Chloride), is fine for cold-water lines anywhere inside or outside the house. Maximum working temperature is 150° F. PVC pipe is made in both light-duty solvent-welded pipe and fittings or in heavy-duty Schedule 40 pipe. The latter is used mostly for irrigation work. The former could well be used for all cold water lines in the house. PVC water-supply sizes are less costly than CPVC and sizes go along steel-pipe diameters, thus giving a larger pipe passageway. Fittings are limited to the basic ones that adapt, reduce, couple, bend, and connect. PVC pipe comes in 20-foot lengths. Use only PVC solvent for making the solvent-welded joints.

POLYETHYLENE PIPE

Still another useful plastic pipe is PE (PolyEthylene). Being flexible and furnished in long coils, it is especially useful for underground water-supply lines from water main to house. Size is based on inside diameter and it comes in ½, ¾, 1-inch and larger. Fittings consist of adapters to inside and outside threads, couplings, elbows, and tees. Fittings are either of molded polystyrene plastic or made of galvanized steel. The pipe slips over serrated fittings and is clamped with stainless steel band screw clamps. PE pipe is available in wall thickness for 80 psi, 100 psi, 125 psi and 160 psi. If it is to be used for your water supply, it should be rated by the National Sanitation Foundation. (The same is true of any pipe and fittings you use for that purpose.) All PE pipes so rated are stamped with the letters *NSF*.

A prime use for PE pipe is to bring the water up from a well. The 125 psi pipe will withstand 150 safely. It is also an excellent choice for an underground service line for the well or water main to the house.

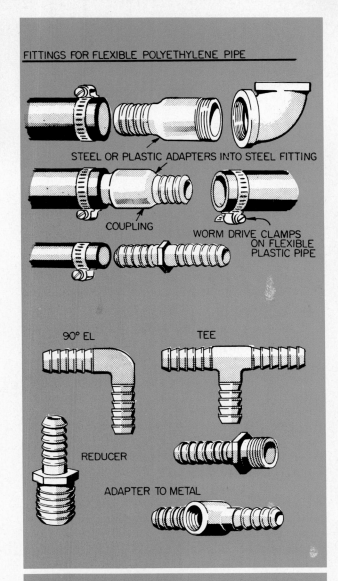

FITTINGS FOR FLEXIBLE POLYETHYLENE PIPE

STEEL OR PLASTIC ADAPTERS INTO STEEL FITTING

COUPLING

WORM DRIVE CLAMPS ON FLEXIBLE PLASTIC PIPE

90° EL

TEE

REDUCER

ADAPTER TO METAL

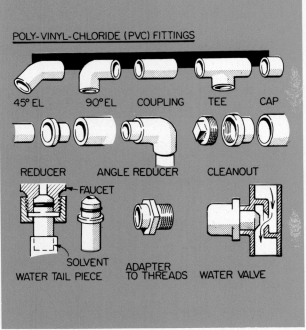

POLY-VINYL-CHLORIDE (PVC) FITTINGS

45° EL   90°EL   COUPLING   TEE   CAP

REDUCER   ANGLE REDUCER   CLEANOUT

FAUCET

SOLVENT WATER TAIL PIECE

ADAPTER TO THREADS

WATER VALVE

Plastic DWV pipe is a natural for prefabrication of components on the floor. Its quick-drying solvent-welded joints let an entire section of the DWV system be assembled in just a few minutes.

Plastic Drain Waste Vent Pipe

If your code permits, plastic is the easiest to use and the most economical DWV pipe you can buy. Efficient, too.

PLASTIC PIPE IN DWV sizes comes in either of two materials: PVC and ABS (Acrylonitrile-Butadiene-Styrene). PVC drain-waste-vent pipe, like PVC water-supply pipe, is light in color; ABS is black. PVC solvent welding cement is used to join PVC DWV pipe and fittings. ABS calls for the use of ABS cement, which is black like the pipe. The two pipes (PVC and ABS), their fittings and their solvent cements are not interchangeable without using a special solvent. Incidently one pint of solvent will do about 30 3-inch joints or more than 65 1½-inch joints.

PVC pipe has been widely used in Europe for years and is also found in the East and Midwest but ABS pipe seems to be a requirement in the western United States. Either will do the job, but you have to use what your code permits.

PVC DWV pipe and fittings in the 3-inch soil-stack size by Genova have a big advantage over ABS. They are designed to fit completely within a standard 3½-inch stud wall. ABS pipe and fittings, though their nominal size is also 3 inches, are larger on the outside. To use them requires furring the wall out an extra inch.

Plastic DWV pipes and fittings have the benefit of being lightweight, thus needing less support from the house framing. No flame is needed to join them, and that danger is avoided. One minor drawback is they can be easily penetrated by nails. The plastic also may be affected by certain chemical solvents, but how often do

Below. Can you believe, these are the only tools you'll need on plastic drain-waste-vent pipe. Brush should be about half the diameter of the pipe. That, plus a saw and knife is all you need.

Look for the designation on each plastic Drain-Waste-Vent fitting to be sure it's rated for such use. It should state "DWV" on both pipe and fittings. If not, it is intended for underground use.

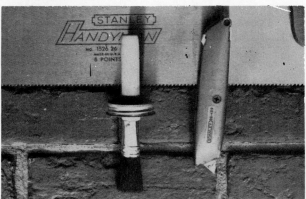

Difference between ABS, DWV pipe (top) and thinner-walled Genova PVC (bottom) enables pipe with fittings to fit within a standard 2 x 4 stud wall. Larger ABS pipe requires furring out.

you pour methyl-ethyl-ketone down your drains? Chemical drain cleaners, soaps, detergents, and the like—as used at home—have no harmful effect on plastic.

One last drawback that may—or may not—affect you. In some areas of the country rodents have actually eaten a section to a point where it required replacement!

Solvent-welded saddle tee is a handy fitting for adding onto plastic DWV systems (where code permits). To use it locate, mark and cut out existing stack; then weld saddle tee over the cutout.

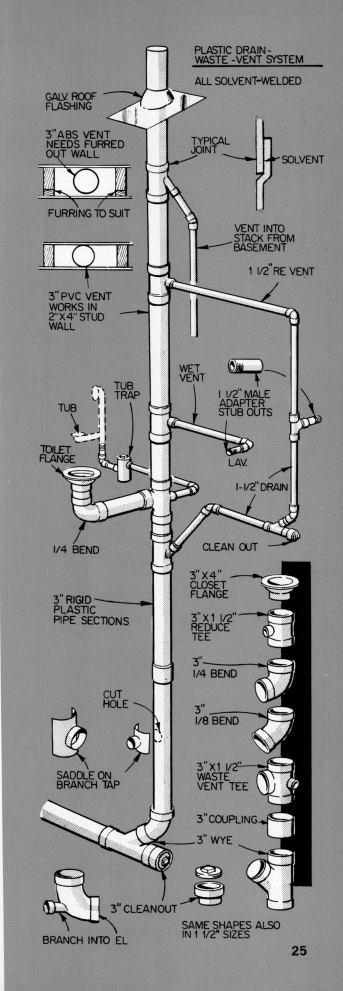

PLASTIC DRAIN-WASTE-VENT SYSTEM
ALL SOLVENT-WELDED

GALV. ROOF FLASHING

3" ABS VENT NEEDS FURRED OUT WALL

FURRING TO SUIT

3" PVC VENT WORKS IN 2"X4" STUD WALL

TYPICAL JOINT

SOLVENT

VENT INTO STACK FROM BASEMENT

1 1/2" RE VENT

TUB TRAP

TUB

WET VENT

1 1/2" MALE ADAPTER STUB OUTS

TOILET FLANGE

LAV.

1-1/2" DRAIN

1/4 BEND

CLEAN OUT

3" RIGID PLASTIC PIPE SECTIONS

3" X 4" CLOSET FLANGE

3" X 1 1/2" REDUCE TEE

3" 1/4 BEND

3" 1/8 BEND

3" X 1 1/2" WASTE VENT TEE

CUT HOLE

SADDLE ON BRANCH TAP

3" COUPLING

3" WYE

3" CLEANOUT

BRANCH INTO EL

SAME SHAPES ALSO IN 1 1/2" SIZES

Other Types of Pipe

This "catch-all" section deals with other kinds of pipe you may need in or around your home.

Advanced Drainage Systems corrugated lightweight underground pipes come in rolls and 10' lengths that can be carried even in your subcompact. No need for tieing red flags behind.

New easy-to-do PVC pipe for house-to-sewer connections and septic-system watertight lines is called Ring-Tite by Johns-Manville. Locked-in rubber sealing ring lets you join pipes in seconds.

WE'VE SAVED THIS SPOT for a description of the other kinds of pipe you can get. Clear vinyl tubing is good for serving humidifiers and water coolers. It uses standard compression fittings except that a plastic ferrule is installed over the tube end instead of a brass one, as with copper tubing. Vinyl tubing is so light and flexible it can run anywhere where it will be free from physical damage. It is also cheaper than copper tubing of the same size.

UNDERGROUND DRAINAGE

A number of different pipe types are used for underground outside-the-home drainage of sewage, roof runoff water, and ground water. While DWV pipes and fittings could be used, lower-cost underground pipes may substitute. Sizes are 3- and 4-inch ID; lengths are mostly 10 feet. Underground plastic pipe does not bear the DWV or Schedule 40 designation, and should never be used indoors, except, perhaps, for underfloor basement drainage into a sump pit.

Here are the kinds of underground pipe you should know about:

PVC ABS—made of the same materials as the DWV piping, they are light in weight and easy to join with solvent-welded couplings. Perforated pipe is available for seepage-trench use.

RS—Rubber-styrene pipe works pretty much

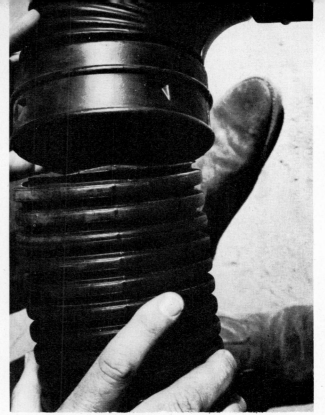

Seepage pipe in the Advanced System may be had either in the usual perforated pipes or in slotted pipes as here. Saw cuts spaced like perforations let water out as it flows along pipe.

Advanced Systems ¼ bend snaps onto the end of a length of pipe. Corrugations permit the pipe to be made of very light gauge plastic yet still withstand backfill pressures. Pipe is not for sewers.

the same as the above pipes. Use ABS cement to join RS pipes and fittings. Diameter is 4 inches. Perforated RS pipe is available.

PITCH-FIBER—Old and reliable, pitch-fiber, or bituminous, pipe goes together with tapered couplings. The joints are tapped together to hold. Diameter is 3 or 4 inches, and perforated, as well as solid-wall pipe is available. For less than full lengths, a taper-jointing field lathe is needed. Try renting it where you buy the pipe.

VITRIFIED-CLAY—If you use vitrified-clay pipe, get the kind with self-joints using either neoprene rubber gaskets or asphalt solvent-welded joints. It comes in 4-inch and larger diameters, 2-foot and 5-foot lengths. Use foot-long clay or concrete field tiles where seepage is wanted.

ADS SYSTEM—This patented corrugated plastic pipe is so light in weight that you can carry an entire septic field installation in one coil. Pipe and fittings snap together through their formed corrugations. Available solid-wall or slotted for seepage. If your dealer doesn't have it, write Advanced Drainage Systems, Inc., Box 489, Pomona, California 91769, for information on where to buy it. Many codes haven't accepted it yet for sewerage work but it should be okay anywhere for handling surface water.

Short lengths of extruded clay pipe or cast concrete (as shown above) are popular in seepage fields and to drain off water accumulating around a footing. Wear gloves when you work.

Bituminous (pitch-fiber) pipe simplifies the problem of foundation drainage, leader runoff and dispersement of sewage effluent. Check your building code for use as a sewer connection.

To make a calked joint in hub-and-spigot cast iron pipe, first pack rope oakum into the joint. Ram it down hard with the offset calking tool. Pack tightly, but leave it about 1″ below the hub.

Melt one pound of lead per inch of joint in a ladle. While still hot, pour the molten lead in to fill joint. Asbestos joint-running tool and clamp holds the lead in joints on horizontal runs.

WORKING WITH PIPE: Cast Iron

Like brass pipe in water lines, cast iron has been time-tested as the most permanent Drain-Waste-Vent system. But something new has been added.

WIDELY RECOGNIZED as the best drain-waste-vent piping is cast iron. Until recently, the common joining method required for cast iron pipe was by stuffing rope oakum around the joint, packing it in place then pouring in lead. This was hard work, troublesome, and not well suited to do-it-yourself. So cast iron piping was something the pros installed. Now, though, the industry is well along with the use of No-Hub pipe, so called by the Cast Iron Soil Pipe Institute. It is such a great method for joining these heavy pipes that the pros use it widely.

Instead of having a bell-and-spigot design built into the pipe ends and fittings, No-Hub pipes and fittings are plain-ended. To make a joint, the ends are slipped into a neoprene rubber sleeve and a stainless steel shield is slipped over the sleeve and tightened at both ends with screw clamps. The resulting joint is somewhat flexible yet leakproof. Only one tool is needed:

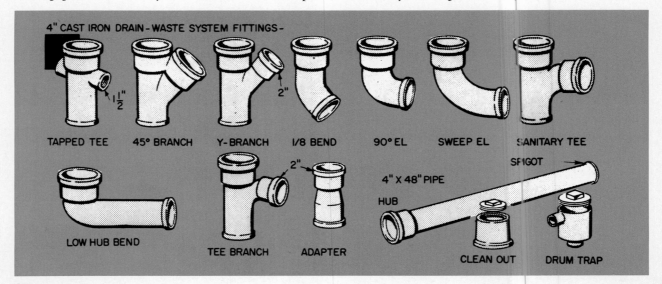

4" CAST IRON DRAIN-WASTE SYSTEM FITTINGS-

TAPPED TEE   45° BRANCH   Y-BRANCH   1/8 BEND   90° EL   SWEEP EL   SANITARY TEE

1½"   2"

LOW HUB BEND   TEE BRANCH   ADAPTER   2"

4" X 48" PIPE   HUB   SPIGOT

CLEAN OUT   DRUM TRAP

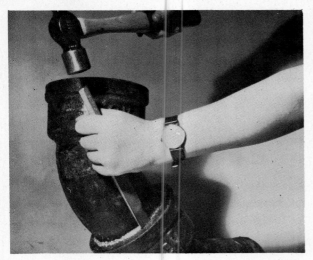

Pack the cooled lead against the hub and pipe with the calking tool. If you get a dual-purpose flattened tool, it can do both jobs. Angled-end tools require one for hub, another for the pipe.

a 60-inch-pound torque wrench for tightening. Unless you have a lot of work to do, tightening can be handled with a 5/16-inch socket wrench.

A WAY OUT

In practical application, there is no space between the joints and none need be allowed for. This simplifies pipe assembly and minimizes errors. If an error is made with No-Hub, the joint can be taken apart in seconds and the error corrected by cutting or by installing a longer pipe.

Just as easily, the system can be opened up for adding onto the DWV system. And when adding onto an old cast iron DWV system, the best way is to cut out the necessary amount of old pipe, leaving plain ends on the pipe at either end and simply install a new hubless fitting. A tee or wye, or whatever is wanted, can be installed in this way. But you will find the hardest part is cutting out the old pipe.

USE ANYWHERE

Hubless pipe comes in 2-, 3-, and 4-inch diameters and 5-foot and 10-foot lengths. Diameters are ID. All can be adapted to fixture traps, toilets, sewer pipes with available adapters and couplings. Branch drains of less than 2 inches are made with 1½-inch galvanized steel pipe and drainage-type threaded fittings used in the No-Hub tappings.

No-Hub pipe and fittings may be used above or below ground. You can run it all the way to the sewer, if you wish. Like all cast iron pipe, it is crushproof, and resistant to solvents, acids, everything. Cast iron pipe needs no protection

LEADED JOINTS

To make a leaded joint, stuff rope oakum around the joint, packing it very tightly. In fact, the oakum should be tight enough to hold the joint by itself. Pound the oakum down with a joint-calking tool and keep adding more until it comes to ¾ to 1 inch of the top of the hub. Then pour in melted lead to fill the joint. When cooled off, pound the lead down and against the pipe, then against the hub with the calking tool. The resulting joint should be leak-free and tight with no pipe movement possible.

Horizontal joints call for the use of a joint-running tool, an asbestos ring and clamp that holds the molten lead in the joint while it cools. About a pound of lead is needed for each inch of pipe diameter.

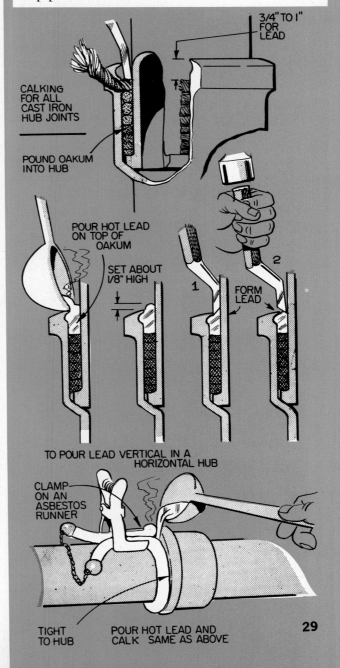

CALKING FOR ALL CAST IRON HUB JOINTS

POUND OAKUM INTO HUB

3/4" TO I" FOR LEAD

POUR HOT LEAD ON TOP OF OAKUM

SET ABOUT I/8" HIGH

1   2
FORM LEAD

TO POUR LEAD VERTICAL IN A HORIZONTAL HUB

CLAMP ON AN ASBESTOS RUNNER

TIGHT TO HUB

POUR HOT LEAD AND CALK SAME AS ABOVE

29

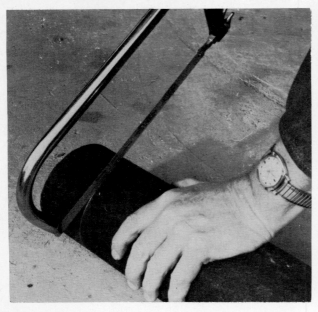

Cutting cast iron soil pipe isn't easy, (unless you can rent a cast iron pipe cutter) but it must be done. Hubless or hub-and-spigot is the same. First saw a 1/16" deep groove around the pipe.

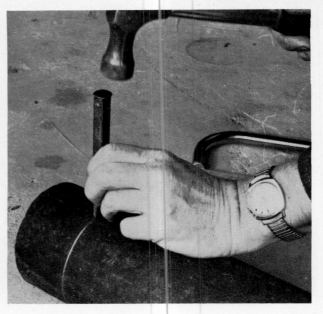

Tap the pipe all around the sawed groove with hammer and cold chisel, hitting harder on every round. When the pipe develops a hollow, dead sound, it's about to break off on the score mark.

from careless nailing. The 3-inch size with fittings can go into a standard stud wall with an inch of furring added. As is the case with conventional cast iron, the No-Hub system is designed to outlast your house. It is ideal for remodeling because of its compatibility with existing cast iron pipe used in many older homes.

Because hubless pipe is cast iron and must be cut with hacksaw and chisel, working with it is not as easy as working with plastic pipe. Still, if you want the very best most flexible system, and are willing to do the cutting, No-Hub is for you. However, the hardest part of the No-Hub job may be getting the pipe and fittings because it is not sold in all outlets.

Once the pipe is cut to the correct length, it is easily joined to a fitting or another length of pipe. No-Hub pipe has the same wall thickness as regular cast iron so both can be easily joined.

No-Hub pipe is made the same way as regular cast iron pipe but does not require the usual lead joint. Instead, joining is made with special Neoprene sleeves held by two stainless steel clamps.

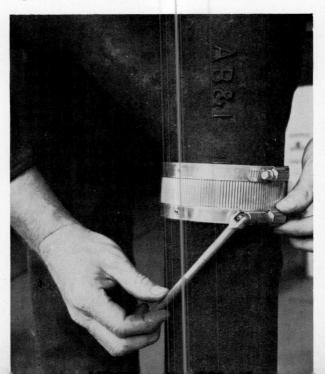

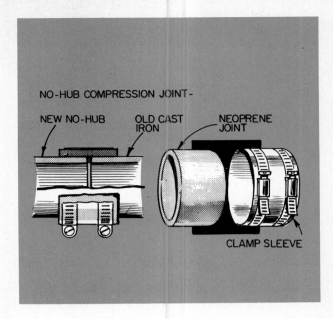

NO-HUB COMPRESSION JOINT

NEW NO-HUB OLD CAST IRON NEOPRENE JOINT

CLAMP SLEEVE

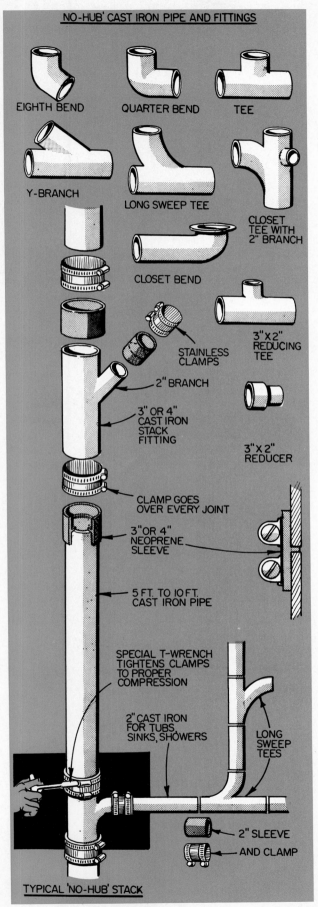

EIGHTH BEND   QUARTER BEND   TEE

Y-BRANCH

LONG SWEEP TEE

CLOSET TEE WITH 2" BRANCH

CLOSET BEND

3"X 2" REDUCING TEE

STAINLESS CLAMPS

2" BRANCH

3" OR 4" CAST IRON STACK FITTING

3"X 2" REDUCER

CLAMP GOES OVER EVERY JOINT

3" OR 4" NEOPRENE SLEEVE

5 FT. TO 10 FT. CAST IRON PIPE

SPECIAL T-WRENCH TIGHTENS CLAMPS TO PROPER COMPRESSION

2" CAST IRON FOR TUBS, SINKS, SHOWERS

LONG SWEEP TEES

2" SLEEVE

AND CLAMP

TYPICAL 'NO-HUB' STACK

IF YOU GO THE HUBLESS route with cast iron DWV pipe, cutting the pipe, as we have said, (unless you can rent one of the new cast iron pipe cutters) is the hardest part of the installation. First figure out how long the pipe should be. If you prop the end fittings in place, you can take a direct measurement. Nothing need be added for makeup, the distance the pipe reaches into the fitting. With No-Hub, pipe ends almost butt together and there need be no makeup allowance.

Mark a line squarely around the pipe with a chalkline. Wrapped around the pipe, it not only gets the line square, but is self-marking. A square cut is important.

Next saw a groove 1/16 to 1/8-inch deep all the way around the pipe and then take a cold chisel and hammer and work around the groove several times hitting harder with each round. When you hear a hollow sound, the pipe is about to break. Don't hit too hard at first, or you're apt to break the pipe away from the line.

NO-HUB JOINT

To join two pipes with the hubless method, place the rubber sleeve on the end of one pipe and the stainless steel shield on the end of the other pipe or on the fitting. Insert the pipe or fitting into the sleeve until the ends butt against the separator ring inside the sleeve. Tighten first one screw clamp then the other, alternating until you tighten to 60-inch pounds torque.

Provide support for horizontal runs of hubless pipe at every joint if the length between hangers would be more than 4 feet. Suspensions more than 18 inches below the supports need sway bracing to keep them from swinging.

31

Tools for easy working with copper pipe are simple and basic. You'll need hacksaw, steel wool (for cleaning ends of pipe and fittings). tubing cutter, propane torch, striker, flaring set.

WORKING WITH PIPE:

Copper Tubing/Pipe

Next to plastic, copper tubing and pipe is the easiest material to work.

HOW YOU INSTALL COPPER tubing depends on what type of joints you plan to use. For DWV copper there is only one kind of joint —sweat-soldered. For water supply tubing you have a choice of sweat-soldered joints, flare or compression fittings. A flare or compression joined copper water-supply system is easy to work on but the cost of the fittings is substantial. So soldered fittings are usually used.

Start by measuring the tubing, the length of the tubing the run requires, allowing extra makeup at each end that is equal to the diameter of the tubing. Thus, add ½ inch at each end when using ½-inch tubing, etc. However, because different fitting manufacturers may have different socket depths, it is best to check the socket depth of the fitting you use and adjust your make-up accordingly.

When cutting the tubing, make certain the cut is square and all burrs are removed from the inside and outside edge. Clean the surface of both the tubing and the inside of the fitting with emery cloth, flux all surfaces and join together. Heat the joint with your torch. Remember, if you get the joint too hot, it will oxidize and cannot be soldered successfully. Pull it apart while still hot, reclean, flux and try again. If the joint is too cold the solder won't flow either. But with a little practice you will know just when you have the correct amount of heat to produce a perfect joint.

The time to fix a poor joint is before you get water in the system. Once you have water in the system, even getting the fitting hot enough to pull apart is difficult because water and steam inside the pipe keep it too cool for the solder to melt. Sometimes the pipe must be sawed apart to let the water and steam out so the fitting can be resoldered. In any case, it is okay to reuse the fitting if you clean it carefully until both the copper and the tinned portions are bright.

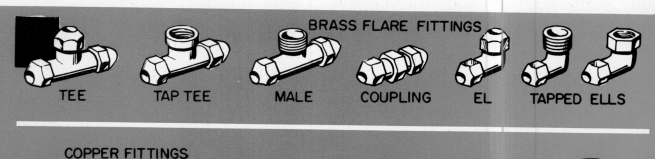

BRASS FLARE FITTINGS

TEE TAP TEE MALE COUPLING EL TAPPED ELLS

COPPER FITTINGS

 EL

 TEE

TO FEMALE

COUPLE

UNION

EARS

 45°

 REDUCER

TO MALE

TAP EL

CAP

STREET EL

Size, inches	Outside Diameter	Inside Diameter	Wall Thickness	Cross Sectional Area	Weight, pounds per lin ft
Physical characteristics of copper tube					
TYPE K				**TYPE K**	
¼	.375	.305	.035	.073	0.145
⅜	.500	.402	.049	.127	0.269
½	.625	.527	.049	.218	0.344
⅝	.750	.652	.049	.334	0.418
¾	.875	.745	.065	.436	0.641
1	1.125	.995	.065	.778	0.839
1¼	1.375	1.245	.065	1.22	1.04
TYPE L				**TYPE L**	
¼	.375	.315	.030	.078	0.126
⅜	.500	.430	.035	.145	0.198
½	.625	.545	.040	.233	0.285
⅝	.750	.666	.042	.348	0.362
¾	.875	.785	.045	.484	0.455
1	1.125	1.025	.050	.825	0.655
1¼	1.375	1.265	.055	1.26	0.884
1½	1.625	1.505	.060	1.78	1.14
TYPE M				**TYPE M**	
⅜	.500	.450	.025	.159	0.145
½	.625	.569	.028	.254	0.204
¾	.875	.811	.032	.517	0.328
1	1.125	1.055	.035	.874	0.465
1¼	1.375	1.291	.042	1.31	0.682
TYPE DWV					
1¼	1.375	1.295	.040	1.32	.65
1½	1.625	1.541	.042	1.87	.81
2	2.125	2.041	.042	3.27	1.07
3	3.125	3.030	.045	7.21	1.69
4	4.125	4.009	.058	12.6	2.87

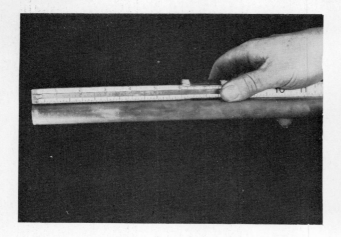

1. Here, step-by-step, is how to make successful sweat-soldered joints in copper tubing. First measure the length of tubing needed, allowing for fitting makeup. Also measure the fitting.

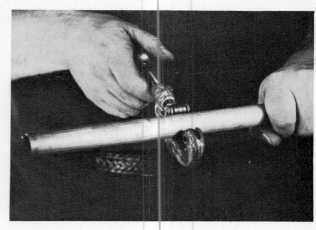

2. Tubing can be cut hand-held if your cutter works easily and you tighten the handle a little at a time. Start the roller right on its mark. Tubing cutters are much better than using hacksaw.

3. Many tubing cutters have a V-shaped reamer built into them for routing out the inside burr left by the cutter. Remember, left-over burr greatly restricts the flow of water through the joint.

4. Use sandpaper, emery cloth or steel wool to clean and brighten the tube end. Clean about ½" beyond the shoulder of the fitting to make certain the solder will flow completely around joint.

5. Fitting socket is brightened with a cleaning tool, as here, or scoured with sandpaper. Be sure to get every part of the fitting socket bright and clean, else the solder may not flow around it.

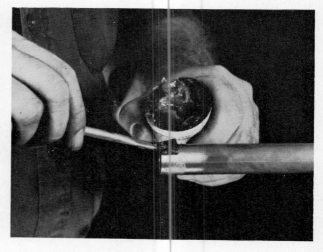

6. Apply non-acid, paste-type soldering flux to the end of the pipe all around. The purpose is to prevent the cleaned copper from oxidizing when it is heated and before any lead solder is applied.

7. Flux the fitting socket the same as the tube end. If you wish, you can prepare and flux several joints on one fitting before soldering. This lets a fitting be heated once to solder its joints.

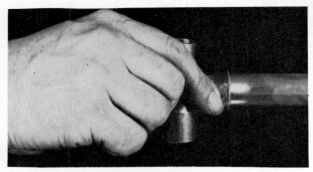

8. Insert the fitting over the pipe to full depth and align it at the permanent angle required. Make sure the pipe is cleaned well beyond the fitting, otherwise the solder may resist flowing.

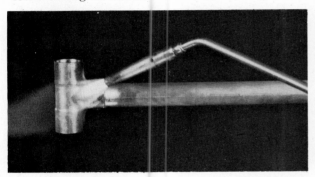

9. When running water lines, a propane torch is ideal. Heat the tubing first, about ½″ from the fitting, playing the flame at right angle to the tubing. Keep the flame in motion.

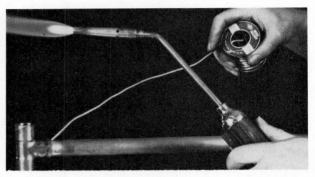

10. With the fitting and tube heated enough to melt the solder freely, feed solder at the joint. Capillary action will actually pull the solder around the fitting joint, even when vertical.

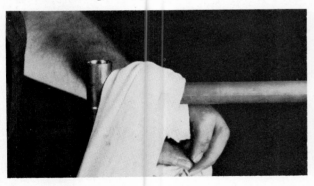

11. Quickly, before the solder cools, wipe round the joint with a soft cloth. This takes off the excess solder and smooths what's left on the joint. It produces a much more workmanlike job.

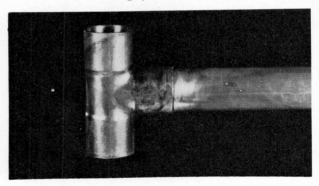

12. The completed sweat-soldered joint, if properly made, should be strong and leak-free. But it's hard to tell by looking, because a good joint may or may not have a solder fillet around it.

A good way to work with copper is to clean, flux and pre-assemble several joints, then solder them in production line fashion. This way an entire tee fitting, for instance, can be soldered with one heat-up.

Soldering DWV piping calls for lots of heat. You'll need one or two gasoline blow torches. The small propane torches will not heat these larger joints sufficiently. Also, when soldering valves, remove the stem to protect the delicate washer from being damaged by heat.

FLARING

Flared joints in soft-tempered copper water tubing are easy to make with a flaring tool. Two types of flaring tools are available, the knock-in kind or the clamping kind. With either one, be sure to install the flare nut on the tube facing out *before* you make the flare.

To use the knock-in type, insert the right-sized tool in the end of the tube and tap it in until the flare is made. With the clamp-type

1. Impact and screw-type flaring tools are used for flaring soft tubing. The impact tool is machined from steel, is most economical. Remove all burrs and then slip the coupling nut on tube.

2. Insert the flaring tool into the pipe end and hammer the tool to produce the desired flare. Do not hold the tube in a vise; you can do it easily hand held. A dozen or so light strokes do the job.

3. Assemble the joint by placing the fitting squarely against the flare. Engage the coupling nut with the fitting threads. Tighten with two wrenches, one on the nut and one on the fitting.

4. Screw-type flaring tools are more expensive but can handle different size tubing. With coupling nut on, clamp the tube in the flaring block so the end extends slightly past the face of block.

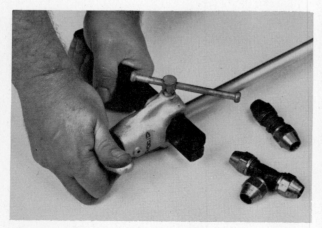

5. Place the yoke of the flaring tool on the block so the beveled end of the compressor cone is over the tube end. Tighten firmly so the tube will not move when the screw is turned

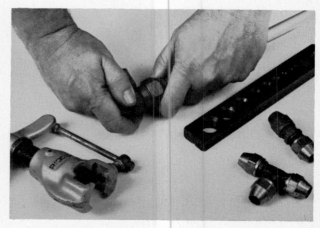

6. Continue to turn the compressor screw until it bottoms out. Then remove and assemble the connection as in Photo 3. Flared joints will withstand greater pressure than soldered joints.

tool, fasten the tube into the clamp with no more than 1/16 inch protruding from the tapered-seat side of the tool. Then screw the cone clamped down into the end of the tube until it seats hard. Unclamp everything and the flare is ready for use.

Compression fittings need no tools other than a pair of wrenches to tighten them. To make one up, slip on the compression nut facing out, then install the brass ferrule onto the end of the tube, allowing about 1/8 inch of tubing to extend beyond the ferrule. Slip the tube into the compression fitting, tighten with one wrench while holding the fitting with another and the job is done. The ferrule is squeezed down around the tube to form a tight seal.

HANGING COPPER RUNS

Support horizontal runs of copper water tubes and DWV lines from every other joist. Supports should be made of copper or copper-plated steel to prevent bimetallic action. Or copper pipe clamps can be used.

BENDING COPPER

You can bend flexible copper tubing most easily around a form. Even your knee will do but be careful not to make the bends too sharp else the tubing will kink. Kinks restrict water flow and may even close the tube off entirely. If you want smooth, tight bends, fit a bending spring over the tube, then bend. Filling the tube with sand works, too, though it is more trouble.

Tight, neat bends can be made in soft-temper copper tubing using a bending tool. With the right-sized tool's handle at 180°, insert the tube in the forming shoe at the point you want it bent.

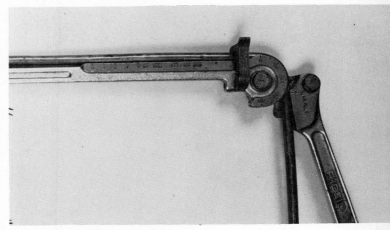

Bend by pulling the handles toward each other, slowly, until you get the angle of bend desired. This is shown on the calibrated forming wheel. Remove tube by opening tool and disengaging.

Three flexible copper connectors are available to help you align lengths of rigid tube. Top has threaded ends. Center one sweat-solders between fittings. Bottom solders between pipes.

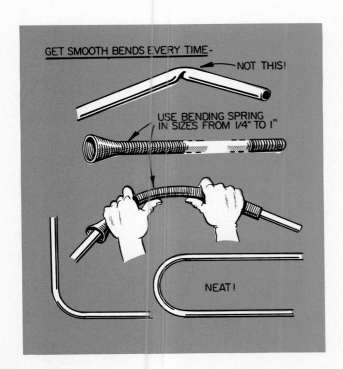

GET SMOOTH BENDS EVERY TIME—
NOT THIS!
USE BENDING SPRING IN SIZES FROM 1/4" TO 1"
NEAT!

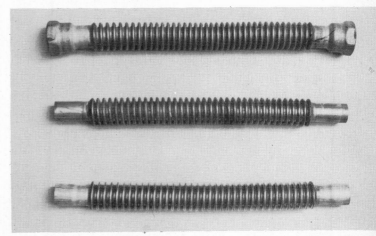

Threaded Pipe

If your code insists upon galvanized steel, black iron or brass pipe, you'll need some special tools and a little know-how.

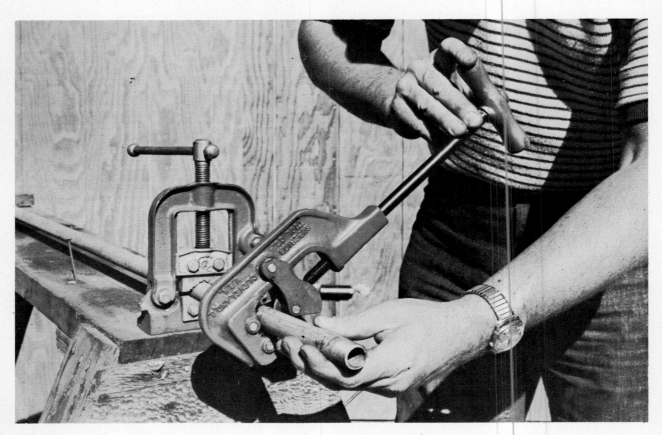

1. To cut and thread galvanized steel pipe to length, clamp it in a pipe vise and start the pipe cutter with its wheel on the cut mark. Rotate the cutter, keep tightening handle until pipe severs.

WORKING WITH THREADED pipes calls for a few specialized tools. If you plan to do much piping, buy a set of tools. If not, you can rent what you need, including a large, portable pipe vise for holding the pipe.

While galvanized steel, black iron, and brass pipe can be cut with a hacksaw, you'll do better with a pipe-cutting tool. It is easier than sawing and always makes a square cut.

FITTING MAKEUP

Before you cut, be sure the length is right. Fitting makeup distance—distance the pipe screws into the fitting—varies with pipe size.

If you measure face-to-face of the fittings, only these makeup measurements need be

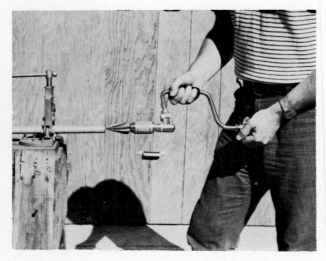

2. Run a tapered pipe reamer into the end of just-cut pipe to remove the burr left by the cutter. Keep reaming until surface is smooth. If left, the burr will restrict the flow of water.

added to the result. If the measurement is from center-to-center of two pipes and must include the fitting, then you must subtract for the distance covered by the fittings. The best way to do this is to lay the fitting out and actually measure.

Here are the usual threaded-pipe makeup allowances:

½-inch pipe— ½ inch
¾-inch pipe— ½ inch
1-inch pipe—9/16 inch
1½-inch pipe—5/8 inch
2-inch pipe—11/16 inch

3.   Now you're ready to cut threads in the pipe. Start the right-sized pipe guide and die on the pipe, guide end first. Guide it straight on by hand and turn gently until the die takes hold.

4.   Turn the die clockwise, cutting threads as you go. If the die binds at any point, back up a quarter-turn to clear the chips, then proceed. Most stocks take a variety of die and guide sizes.

5.   About every turn of the die, stop and squirt some thread-cutting oil on the pipe through openings in the die. If you try to cut without oil, you may tear the threads or break the die.

6.   Now release the pipe from the vise. Pipe vises are especially good for cutting and threading because they are designed to keep from crushing pipe. They also open out for easy assembly.

7.   Wipe the threads clean and inspect them. If you've been successful, the threads should be sharp and complete all the way around with no pieces missing. Thread one turn past the die end.

Teflon tape is a new replacement for pipe dope. It costs more but is not messy. Wrap a single layer clockwise around threads, pulling tight as shown.

Where possible, hold the pipe in a vise and then screw on the fitting. Start the fitting on the threads slowly, and if it doesn't catch check for burrs.

TYPICAL PROCEDURE

Clamp the pipe in a vise. Don't use a metal-working vise because it tends to squeeze the pipe out of shape. Some, however, have separate jaws for clamping pipes, which may be used. Cut with a pipe cutter and then remove the burr inside the pipe with a pipe reamer or round file. If you leave a burr, it will restrict the flow of water through the pipe. If you use a rachet type pipe threading stock, put the right-sized pipe die into one side of the pipe stock. The printing should face out, not in. Install the matching pipe guide in the other side. Size is stamped on each. Tighten the hold-in bolts.

Start the guide onto the pipe and set the stock's ratchet for clockwise rotation. Push the die onto the pipe and ratchet several times around until the threads are well started. Squirt cutting oil generously onto the end of the pipe. Rotate the die, oiling more with every turn. If the die binds, back it off a quarter turn to clear chips.

Makeup, in any pipe, is the distance the pipe goes into the fitting. In this case the 3″ nipple will extend ½″ into the fitting. Since dimensions of fittings may vary, always check the face-to-face and face-to-centerline measurements before you cut and thread. If you cut your pipe too long you may not be able to trim off less than 1″ with a pipe cutter and must use a hacksaw.

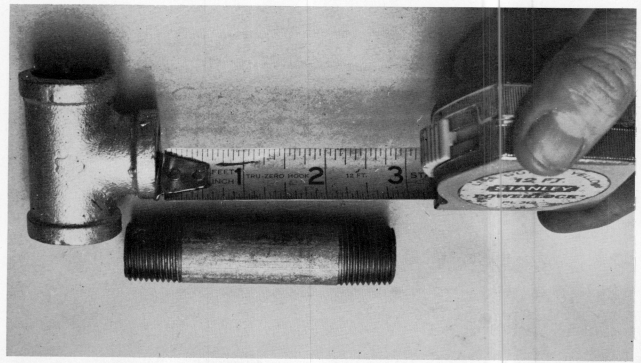

Most fittings have been tightened enough when two or three threads still show. With fittings that have been used once make an extra turn.

Keep going one full turn past the point where the end of the pipe emerges from the die. Stop, reverse the ratchet and back the cutter off. The threads should be clean, sharp and continuous with no broken ones along the way. Broken threads indicate not enough cutting oil, or a worn-out die. Wipe the threads free of excess cutting oil and chips.

INSTALLING FITTINGS

If a fitting is to be installed on the pipe, it can be done easiest with the pipe still in the vise.

Some joint material should be used between pipe threads and fitting threads. It not only enables them to be screwed tighter but, if necessary, it lets them be removed easily. Plumber's pipe dope is commonly used. It comes in stick or putty form. Apply it to the male pipe threads, never to the fitting. Easy and clean to use is TFE pipe tape. It is made of Teflon, the same material that is used to coat easy-clean pots and pans. Wrap a single layer of TFE tape around the pipe threads in a clockwise direction, stretching the tape so that the thread pattern shows through. Install the fitting over the tape.

Tighten the fitting with a pipe wrench pulling the handle toward the open jaws not away from them. This way the teeth bite and hold. Pulled the other way, the wrench only slips. If the pipe is not held in a vise, keep it from turning by holding it with another pipe wrench facing in the opposite direction. You may turn either the pipe or the fitting, whivhever is free to move. Keep going until the fitting is tight. Usually this occurs when only two or three threads are left exposed beyond the fitting. Since pipe threads are tapered, if you go too far, you can split the fitting.

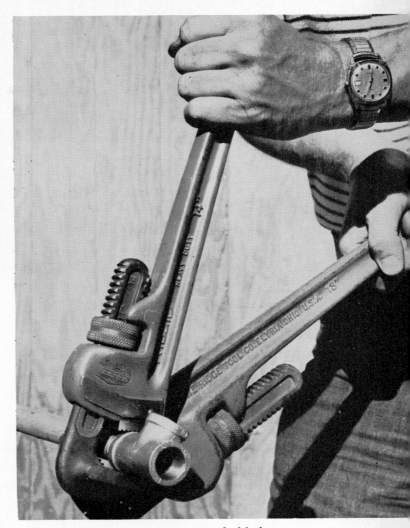

When adding to an existing run, hold the pipe in place with one wrench while you tighten the fitting with a second wrench. It is not necessary to tighten the fitting as far as it will go.

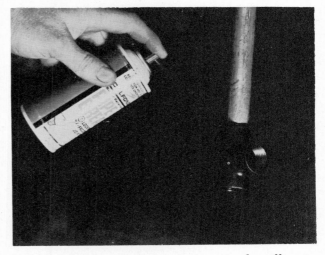

If normal muscle and a long wrench will not move an old fitting, try dabbing or spraying the joint with penetrating oil or some of the handy new products available for just this purpose.

Plastic Pipe

As long as you're going to be working with pipe, why not work with the pipe that works with you? That's plastic! It's easy making watertight joints.

Two-part welded joint system consists of a cleaner that is applied first, followed by the cement. Carefully applied according to instructions, it will produce a joint stronger than the pipe.

PLASTIC PIPE with solvent-welded joints goes together so easy that it is not hard to make mistakes. Count one-two-three before you start the put-together process and you should come out okay.

In measuring for plastic pipe, make allowance for pipe-into-fitting makeup. Measure the fittings you are using, because socket depth varies.

Cutting plastic pipes is best done with a fine-toothed saw in a miter box to make certain the edge is square. The burr left inside the pipe after sawing can be shaved away quickly with a knife; the one outside the pipe can be taken off by sanding.

Test-fit the pipe dry into its fitting; it should enter and slip on tight enough so the fitting won't fall off when held facing down.

SOLVENT-WELDING

Take apart and wipe the pipe and fitting clean. If you use Genova two-part joint cement, apply the cleaner with the brush provided. This step prepares the surfaces for bonding. Then apply a heavy coat of CPVC solvent-welding cement to the pipe end, and a light coat to the inside of the fitting. Don't leave any of the mating surfaces uncoated. Do just one joint at a time. That is all anyone can handle. Also, close

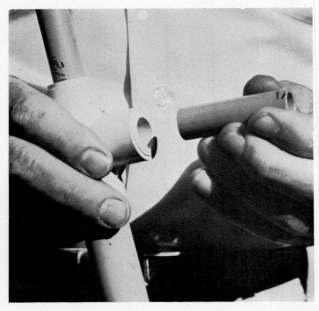

Plastic pipe is light, clean, smooth-walled, and easy to work with. It is a good idea to test the pipe in the fitting before solvent-welding the two. It should slip in, but not fall out.

the solvent can afterward to prevent any thickening.

Now comes the critical part of the job. Be quick. You have less than a minute. Immediately after coating the fitting, slide it onto the end of the pipe with a twist until it bottoms. Adjust the direction exactly as it should face, then hold it there for ten seconds. That's it. Some directions say to forget the holding. You can try it and see how it goes.

CHECK INSIDE

If properly made, the joint should show a fillet of dissolved plastic all around the edge. The solvent should not be so thickly applied that it blocks the pipe passage. Reach a finger in through the fitting and check. If there is any excess cement, pull it out of the pipe and use less solvent next time. If there is no fillet all around, use more solvent next time.

Within 30 seconds a joint is pretty well set. After an hour it is ready to take water pressure.

Never try to move the fitting after a few seconds. If it is in the wrong position, cut it off and start over with another fitting. If you move it, you'll destroy the rapidly developing bond.

Brush size is important in solvent-welding. The brushes and daubers that come with cans of solvent are fine for doping water-supply pipes. But for doping larger DWV pipes you need a larger brush. Ideal brush width is half the pipe diameter. Either use a paint brush (a cheapie that you can discard) or buy one of the special can-top brushes made for this purpose.

In addition to a clean and burr-free end, when the pipe is cut to length the cut must be square. If you don't have a fancy miter-box like this one buy a simple wooden one. Use a back or hack saw.

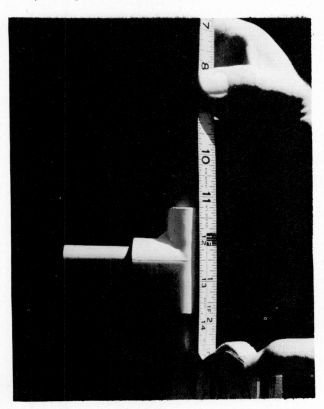

As in the case of copper sweat fittings, the inside dimensions of fittings by different manufacturers are not the same. So check the make-up depth of each fitting before you cut your pipe.

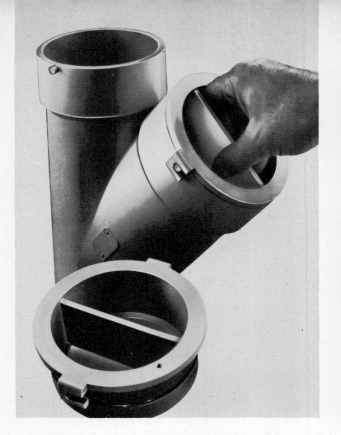

For making cleanouts in plastic drain-waste-vent systems, a new product by Genova does it best. Instead of threaded cleanout covers—which tend to stick—it uses twist-lock covers with O-rings.

Genova Pop-Top toilet flange seals off the toilet opening in a DWV system for water-testing. Left in place until you are ready to install the toilet, it keeps debris out of the system until completion.

They take the place of the dauber supplied with the larger cans of solvent cement.

THREADED FITTINGS

Threaded adapter fittings should be tightened with a smooth-jawed open-end wrench or a strap wrench, never a pipe wrench. Use Teflon pipe tape or special plastic-thread dope on the male threader. Never use ordinary pipe dope as it can dissolve plastic.

Plastic pipes need good support or else they will sag. Use plastic or metal hangers to attach them to framing. Horizontal DWV runs need a support every 48 inches, maximum; water-supply runs should be supported on 32-inch centers. Unlike metal pipes, long runs of plastic must not be so tightly fastened to the framing that they cannot slide back and forth with pipe expansion and contraction. Likewise, the ends of runs should be free to move. Special Genova hangers made for CPVC pipe permit bind-free movement. Vertical runs of DWV may be supported by resting the lowest fitting on a wood cross-member or letting one fitting within the run rest on a header in the wall. Two-story installations need a similar support in each floor.

SPECIAL CARE

CPVC pipe needs special care to prevent pressures and temperatures above its limits. Install an extra-long 18-inch air chamber at each fixture. Washing machines need additional protection because their solenoid control valves shut off so quickly. Your washing machine supply should have an air chamber made of ¾ x 18 inch pipe, a size larger than the water supply branch to the washer. Do it by using ¾-inch tees at that point and reducing the branches to ½ inch with bushings.

At the water heater, install 8- to 11-inch long brass pipe nipples in the hot and cold tappings, then adapt them to run plastic pipe. This keeps tank heat from being conducted to the temperature-sensitive plastic pipe. The best water heater setting is low (140°) or medium (160°). You may use the hot (180°) setting if you wish, although it may push the pipes' temperature to its limit.

CODES

Because CPVC hot- and cold-water pipe is not covered in many codes, you'll have to read your local plumbing code and interpret its provisions. If it lists the permissible pipe types but omits CPVC, you might take this to mean that CPVC isn't prohibited. Whether you can get away with that depends on how strictly enforced the provisions are. You can always ask for a variance.

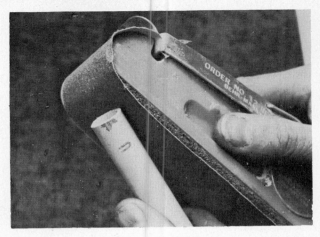

1. Burrs on the outer edge of the pipe are hard to cut off with a knife, so they are removed by lightly sanding the pipe end. A couple of quick passes as you rotate the pipe gets the job done.

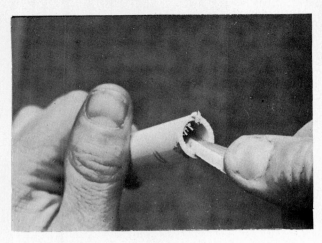

2. Removing the burrs inside a just-cut pipe is important to full flow through the joint, as well as elimination of debris inside the system. It takes a second to slice off burrs with a knife.

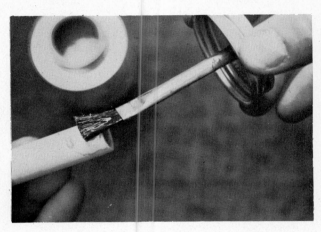

3. If you can use a small brush, you can successfully solvent-weld plastic pipes. Just brush the correct solvent over the last half-inch of pipe end, all around. Be very liberal.

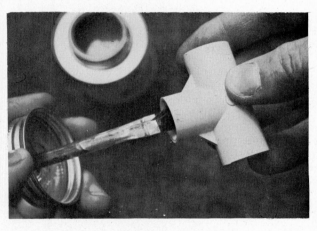

4. Quickly give the fitting a light but thorough coating of solvent full depth of the socket. Too much gunk in the fitting will block the passages. Not enough permits leaks. Check after assembly.

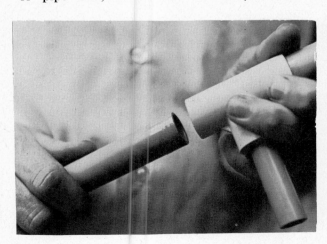

5. Here's how the coated pipe should look before it slips into the coated fitting. Some directions call for giving the pipe a slight twist as it goes in, thus helping to spread solvent evenly.

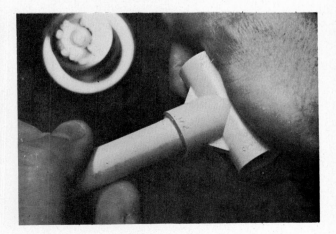

6. Within a few seconds after coating pipe and fitting, insert the pipe into the fitting all the way, align it properly, and hold it there while you count to ten. Keep the solvent can closed.

Install a New Water Heater

The average hot water heater lasts about 7 to 10 years, with a 15-year-life maximum. Here are the replacement techniques.

Four kinds of connections are needed by most water heaters: flue (as above), water, fuel and safety relief. An electric water heater needs no flue. Double-insulated vent can pass near framing.

WHEN YOU NOTICE a puddle of water underneath the water heater, it is time to replace it because it seldom pays to try to patch up an old heater. Chances are that the leak developed in the thinnest spot of the tank and other such spots aren't far behind. By the time you rip off the metal covering, peel away the tank insulation, find and fix the leak, then replace everything again, you've done the work of installing a new heater.

The heater you choose will probably use the same fuel the old one does. Converting from one fuel to another involves a whole new installation, which runs the cost up. But in case you have thought of changing fuels, here are the quantities required to heat an average family's 3000 gallons of hot water each month:

Multiply the figures by the local price of each fuel and you will see what water heating with each type of fuel will cost you every month.

WHAT SIZE WATER HEATER?

Heater size is always a big question. Remember, the actual amount of hot water you can draw in an hour equals 70 per cent of the heater's storage capacity plus its recovery rate. Recovery rate is the number of gallons of water the heater will raise 100° in temperature per hour.

To find your family's hot-water requirements, check the following table.

FIRST-HOUR HOT WATER DELIVERY (Recovery rate plus 70% of storage capacity)	
People in Family	Hot Water Needed
2	45 gal.
3-4	50 gal.
5	60 gal.

The following heaters would do for a family of five with a two-bedroom home and automatic washer and dishwasher: A 30-gallon natural gas heater with a rapid recovery 63 gallon per hour recovery rate; a 50 gallon, LP-gas model with a 38-gph recovery; a 30-gallon oil-fired heater with a 130-gph recovery (oil-fired water heaters have fantastic recovery rates); or a 66-gal. electric heater with dual 4500-watt elements for a 28-gph recovery rate.

HEATER QUALITY

A good water heater with proper care should give 15 years of service. Length of the guarantee is an indication of quality. The best heaters are covered in full—not pro-rated—for ten years.

Of course, your water's corrosive and scale formation properties will affect the tank life. For most waters, a glass lined steel tank is the best choice. It's the industry standard. If you have hard or corrosive water, consider installing water-treatment equipment right along with your new heater.

Only if water treatment is not practical, should you move to a more expensive water heater with a copper tank. Copper forms an oxide coating that is practically impervious to corrosion.

Aluminum-tank water heaters are not recommended. Glass-lined tanks are cheaper and will outlast them. Galvanized steel tanks are cheapest, but are not recommended because they fail much too soon.

INSTALLATION

To install a new heater, turn off the fuel supply to the heater and the cold water supply. Empty the old heater through its drain tap and by opening a hot-water faucet upstairs. Disconnect the pipes leading to the heater while it drains. You're fortunate if unions were provided. Otherwise, cut through the pipes and install unions when replacing them.

If the new heater is higher or lower than the old one, you'll have to modify the plumbing to fit. It is probably best to use the same type of pipe that is already there, thus avoiding too many adapters.

The most important thing to remember about installing any water heater is to see that it is fitted with a temperature-pressure relief (T & P) valve. No water heater is safe without one. New heaters have top tappings for easy installation of T & P valves. All you have to do is thread the valve in and run ¾-inch pipe from it to a convenient drain. The T & P valve prevents your water heater from literally exploding, should all of its energy cutoff features fail. T & P capacity should equal or exceed the heater's BTU-per-hour output. Its temperature-sensing element must be in contact with water in the top 6 inches of the tank.

Every fire-heater installation should include a flue check. Hold a lighted match in the draft diverter or draft regulator opening with the heater's burner operating. The flame should be drawn into the opening.

HEATER CARE

Once a month, after your heater is installed, you should test the T & P valve by lifting up the test lever. If some water is valved off, it is working satisfactorily. Open the heater's drain valve and run off a pail of water to flush any accumulated sediment from the tank. If left, it can harden into an insulating crust that hastens tank burnout.

If your tank has a magnesium anode, it may be used up after some 3 to 10 years of service. Check on it occasionally by screwing it out of the top of the tank.

ELECTRIC HOT WATER

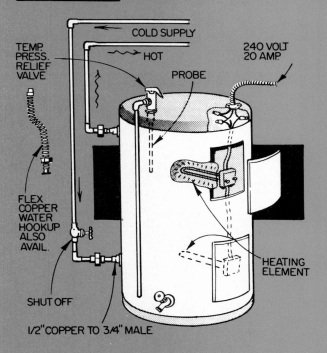

GAS FIRED HOT WATER TANK

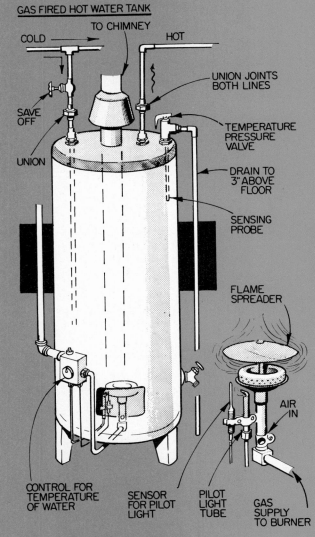

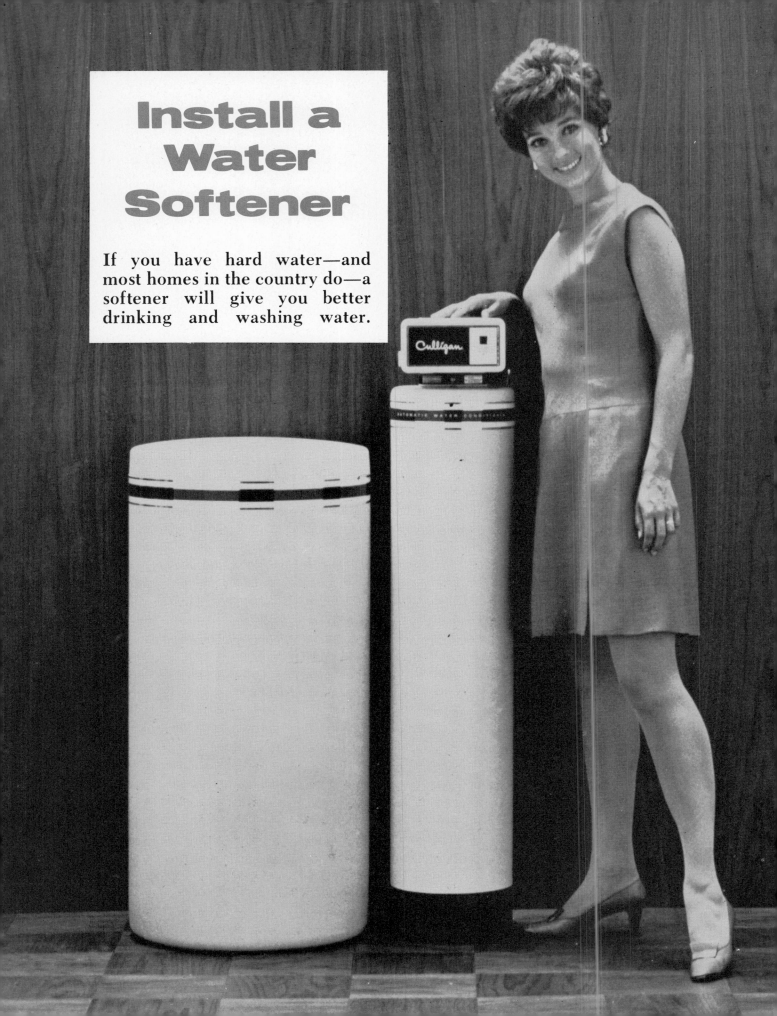

Install a Water Softener

If you have hard water—and most homes in the country do—a softener will give you better drinking and washing water.

Left, modern water softener has a large brine tank for salt and a smaller unit that does the business. Automatic "softness sensors" regenerate the unit, using brine from the big tank

If your water is unpleasant to drink or you need mineral-free water for a diet, reverse-osmosis unit will give it to you., It "filters" out most undesirables with ordinary house water pressure.

RARE IS THE HOUSEHOLD water that cannot be improved by a modern home water-treatment unit. Very often water is hard and hard water forces you to use more soap. Launder in harsh detergents and it leaves the too-familiar bathtub ring. And sometimes it tastes bad. Hardness, sediment, and bad taste are the most frequent complaints. Private water sources can also bring problems of iron, sulfur and bacterial contamination.

Hard water is easy to detect. Soap lathers poorly, then leaves a scummy deposit on clothes, hair, etc. Minerals in it deposit on water heater tanks, cookware, and may even build up to restrict water-supply pipes.

WATER ANALYSIS

The first step in improving your household water is to find out what is wrong with it. Your water company can give you an analysis showing hardness, iron, and other problems. These are measured in grains per gallon (gpg), milligrams per liter (mg/1), the metric measure, or in parts per million (ppm). The following hardness figures are widely accepted.

Grains per gal.	Parts per million	Water Quality
less than 1.0	less than 17.1	soft
1 to 3.5	17.1 to 60	slightly hard
3.5 to 7.0	60 to 120	moderately hard
7.0 to 10.5	120 to 180	hard
10.5 and more	180 and more	very hard

Unless your water rates soft, it can be improved by installing a water softener. Other problems can be corrected, too, sometimes by the softener, or by adding more treatment units ahead of the softener. A softener is always last in line. Your softener can be owned and serviced by a water conditioning service firm or you can buy the softener, install and service it yourself.

REGENERATION

Softeners remove sediment by filtration and get rid of invisible dissolved hardness by a process called ion-exchange. When the ion-exchange mineral's capacity is used up, it is restored by regenerating with softener salt. On the deluxe units, regeneration is done automatically. All you do is keep the salt supply topped

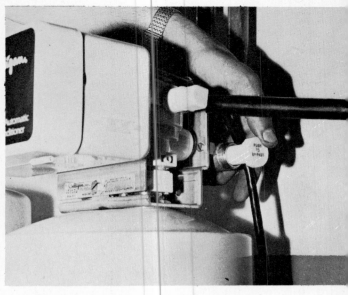

The turn of a dial sets up to date water softener control for either manual or automatic operation. On "automatic" a preset timer makes it regenerate by itself at any predetermined time.

Handy to have on a water softener is a bypass button, especially if outdoor sprinkler is hooked into the softened water. Before sprinkling, push the bypass button to help conserve soft water.

WATER HARDNESS MAP

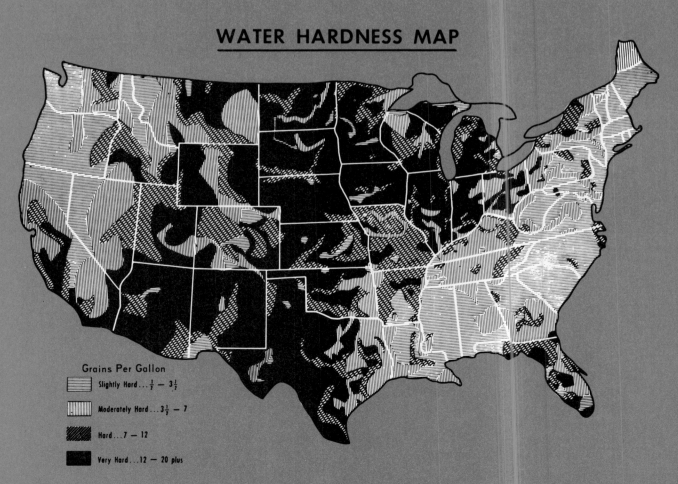

Grains Per Gallon

Slightly Hard... $\frac{1}{2}$ — $3\frac{1}{2}$

Moderately Hard... $3\frac{1}{2}$ — 7

Hard... 7 — 12

Very Hard... 12 — 20 plus

off. A built-in sensor shows the approaching need for regeneration. These automatics are said to save as much as 40 per cent on salt and are especially suited where hardness varies by season.

If your water source is a private well, your softener dealer will make a free water analysis. The standard water softener will remove all hardness, all sediment, and small amounts of iron. If iron content is high, the dealer may recommend using an iron filter.

Combination water softening and chlorine removing appliances are also available. One multipurpose unit removes sediment, hardness and high iron all at once. At any rate, your dealer will advise on what is available to solve your specific water problems. He can also tell you, based on family water use, what size unit you need.

Water softeners are available in appliance-styled cabinets suitable for use in the kitchen,

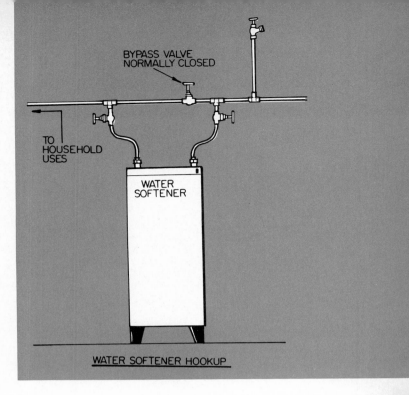

WATER SOFTENER HOOKUP

Below, hard-water scale has made this water heater tank worthless. Mineral build-up holds heat from reaching the water, thus wasting fuel. Softening prevents mineral build-up.

Changing elements in a Culligan water filter is easy as closing a valve and unscrewing the glass container. Element slips out and a fresh one is easily inserted in its place. Filter traps sediment.

Hardly any place in the United States escapes the need for soft water. Darkest areas have the hardest water. Even the lighter areas need water softeners. A simple test will tell about yours.

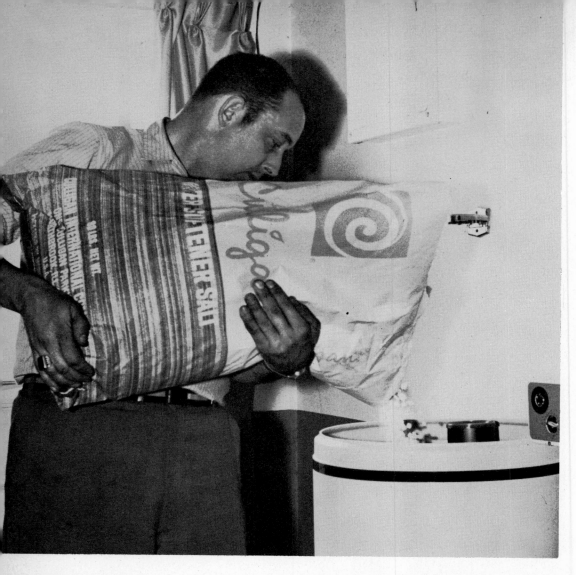

The only attention an automatic home softener needs is keeping it filled with softener salt. Salt usage depends on water usage plus water's hardness. The harder the water the greater quantity used, the more salt must be added to unit.

or in tank-type models for the basement, garage, or utility room installation. If there is space, the two-tank model is best because it gives larger capacity plus a larger salt-storage container. Whatever equipment you buy should bear the seal of the Water Conditioning Foundation.

MAKING THE INSTALLATION

Locating the unit properly is half the job. Give this lots of study. A softener should be piped in series with the house cold-water main. Where you put it depends on whether all water or just some water is to be softened because some families soften only hot water. We recommend that both hot and cold water be softened. Toilet flush water, too. However it is not necessary to soften water that supplies outdoor hose outlets.

To treat all but outdoor water, follow the house water main from the water meter past where the last outdoor supply pipe branches off, but stop before reaching the branches for

Besides not working well with soaps, hard water forms scale inside house piping. As the scale builds, pipe passages narrow. Flow from faucets slows down. Eventually pipes need replacing.

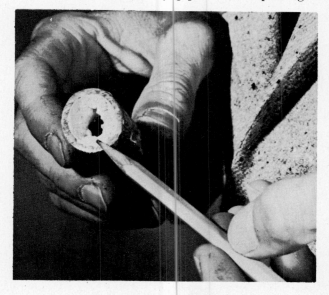

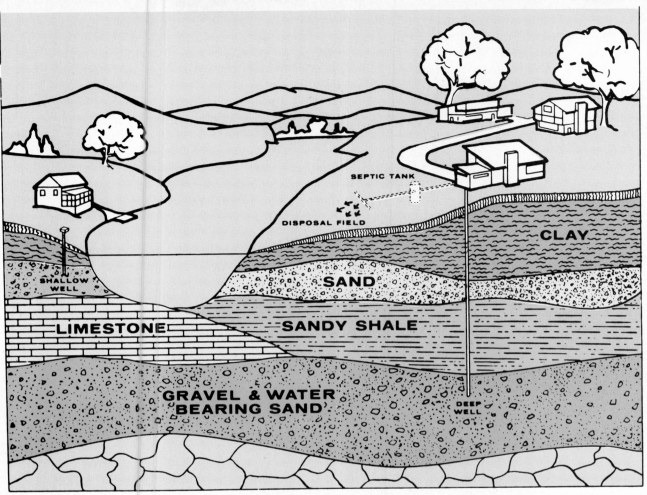

Rain water is soft water. But once it hits the ground it begins dissolving earth minerals and becomes hard. Lake water is ground runoff. Shallow well and deep well may be mineral laden. Test your water first.

any fixture or for the water heater. Connect the softener at this point. If this is not possible, some plumbing revision may be needed to let you water the lawn with hard water.

FLEX-CONNECTORS

Cut through the cold-water main, removing about 8 inches of pipe. Install an elbow on each pipe end. Bring down (or up) pipes from the elbows to the inlet and outlet tappings of the water softener and connect them as described in instructions with the unit. Some provide rubber or copper flexible connections for an easy hookup. Other hookups you'll have to make with pipe. Be sure to install unions on both inlet and outlet pipes so the unit can be removed and replaced easily if necessary without cutting any pipes. You'll also want to install a gate valve in the pipe leading to the inlet side.

For a good installation that will bypass untreated water, with the unit removed, install tees on the cold-water main instead of the elbows. Then reconnect between the tees with

another line that includes a union and a gate valve. Normally closed, this gate valve can be opened with the softener removed to provide your present untreated water service when the softener is removed. This installation also calls for a gate valve in the softener outlet line.

MAINTENANCE

Water softeners all require frequent attention, either by the home owner or by the softener firm. If you do it, what you must do depends on the type of unit and how automatic it is. For a softener the least you do is keep the salt tank filled with softener salt. In all hard-water areas, you can buy rock salt or softener pellets made especially for the purpose. They come in 50-pound rip-top bags. In the ion-exchange process the softener takes hard-water calcium and magnesium out of the water and replaces them with soft-water sodium. When the sodium has all been depleted it must be replaced. Salt—sodium chloride—gives up its sodium to the mineral bed. **53**

A new bathroom vanity cabinet with vitreous china sink top can be installed complete in a few hours. Unit shown above is available to match the decor of any bathroom. It replaced an old free-standing sink.

Replace a Sink or Lavatory

New sinks come in all sizes, shapes and colors. If you're remodeling your bath or kitchen you will want new fixtures. Here's how to install them.

STAINED, CHIPPED, OR DENTED fixtures can make your house look old before its time. The only way to fix them is by replacement. While you are at fixture-changing, you may want to change to one of the good-looking lavatory wood vanity cabinets that not only hide the piping, but provide for towels, soaps, and other bathroom needs.

The new fixture should be centered as nearly as practical on the existing pipes. Most critical is the drain. A trap arm will reach just so far. Moreover, there is a danger of trap siphonage and grease-clogging of the waste pipe, if extended too far.

Sinks always had 1½-inch waste pipes and lavatories 1¼-inch pipes. Now most are installed with 1½-inch piping. The 1¼-inch lavatory trap adapts to the larger waste pipe with a 1¼ x 1½-inch slipnut and washer. If you are working with what is already there, no need to be concerned. Use the same slipnut that you remove.

Countertop sinks and lavatories can be removed without damage to the countertop by taking off the screw clamps from beneath. Then turn off the water to both hot and cold fixture supply pipes and disconnect the faucet hot and cold water ends. Since the wall (or floor) outlets are more accessible than the lower end of the faucet, you may find it easiest to do the removal at this point. Save the fixture supply pipes unless you intend to replace them along with the faucet.

Using a trap wrench or an adjustable pipe or monkey wrench, loosen and remove all the slipnuts on the trap. If they are corroded or resist take-apart, discard the trap for new ones.

Save the dual drain connectors for a two-

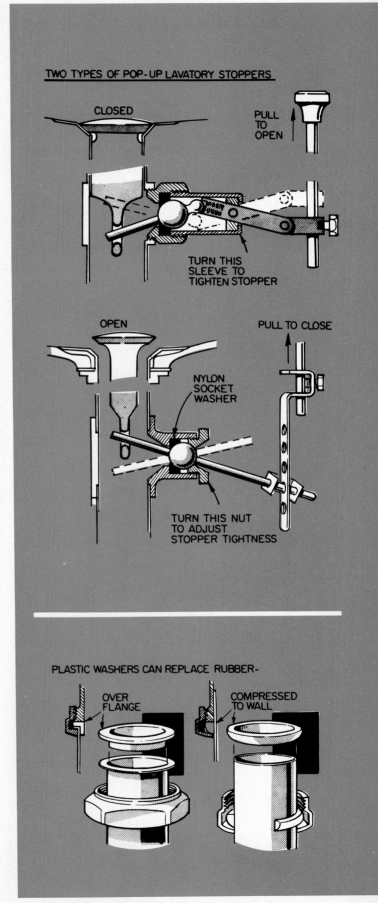

TWO TYPES OF POP-UP LAVATORY STOPPERS

CLOSED

PULL TO OPEN

TURN THIS SLEEVE TO TIGHTEN STOPPER

OPEN

PULL TO CLOSE

NYLON SOCKET WASHER

TURN THIS NUT TO ADJUST STOPPER TIGHTNESS

PLASTIC WASHERS CAN REPLACE RUBBER—

OVER FLANGE

COMPRESSED TO WALL

compartment kitchen sink. Those usually can be re-used. The sink basket drains and lavatory pop-up drain should be discarded along with the old fixture.

The bowl should lift out of the countertop with ease. If not, try prying underneath the trim ring atop the counter.

A wall-hung lavatory merely lifts off of its bracket on the wall. The new one, if the same style, hangs from the same bracket. If you are replacing a wall-hung lavatory with a cabinet-style model, remove the screws in the old bracket and ashcan it, too.

SINK INSTALLATION

If the new countertop sink or lavatory is the same shape and size as the old one, nothing need be done about remodeling the old countertop opening. But if it is larger, the opening should be revised, using the new trim ring as a cutting guide. If the new bowl is smaller, you'll

1. Modern sink faucets, like this Peerless, are designed for easy installation. Faucet's 4″ centers match the hole centers of the fixture bowl. The self-sealing escutcheon needs no putty.

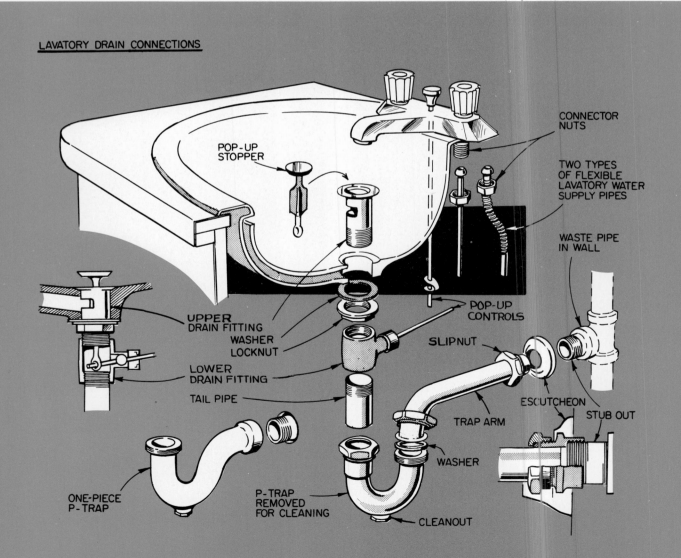

LAVATORY DRAIN CONNECTIONS

POP-UP STOPPER

CONNECTOR NUTS

TWO TYPES OF FLEXIBLE LAVATORY WATER SUPPLY PIPES

WASTE PIPE IN WALL

POP-UP CONTROLS

UPPER DRAIN FITTING

WASHER

LOCKNUT

LOWER DRAIN FITTING

TAIL PIPE

SLIPNUT

TRAP ARM

ESCUTCHEON

STUB OUT

WASHER

ONE-PIECE P-TRAP

P-TRAP REMOVED FOR CLEANING

CLEANOUT

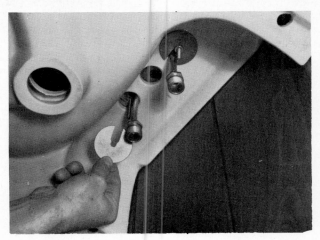

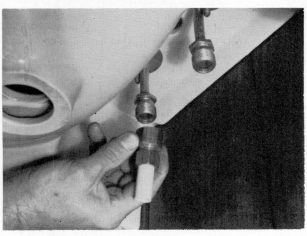

2. From below, slip on a slotted washer provided with the faucet. It fits over the mounting studs and supply pipes. Screw the nut up to hold the faucet tightly on the surface of the fixture.

3. Adapt from the faucet tailpieces to the water-supply system with whatever your dealer recommends for this. Here threaded female CPVC plastic adapters ready tailpieces for pipe.

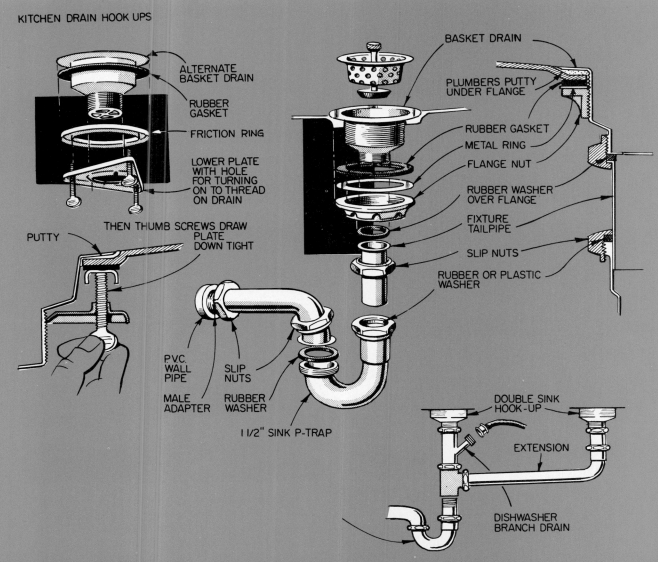

KITCHEN DRAIN HOOK UPS

ALTERNATE BASKET DRAIN

RUBBER GASKET

FRICTION RING

LOWER PLATE WITH HOLE FOR TURNING ON TO THREAD ON DRAIN

THEN THUMB SCREWS DRAW PLATE DOWN TIGHT

PUTTY

P.V.C. WALL PIPE

MALE ADAPTER

SLIP NUTS

RUBBER WASHER

1 1/2" SINK P-TRAP

BASKET DRAIN

PLUMBERS PUTTY UNDER FLANGE

RUBBER GASKET

METAL RING

FLANGE NUT

RUBBER WASHER OVER FLANGE

FIXTURE TAILPIPE

SLIP NUTS

RUBBER OR PLASTIC WASHER

DOUBLE SINK HOOK-UP

EXTENSION

DISHWASHER BRANCH DRAIN

have to build a whole new countertop, cutting the opening according to the new bowl's trim ring.

A cabinet-style unit can be fastened right up to the wall. Attach it to the floor with four steel angle-brackets and screws, and to the wall with four wall anchors. Mount the bowl and secure, using the hardware provided with the cabinet-bowl assembly.

A countertop sink or lavatory mounts the same way as the old one. Have a helper hold the bowl and trim ring in position in the countertop while you reach underneath and insert several screw clamps at intervals around the ring. Install the rest of the screw clamps and tighten them snugly but not enough to distort the trim ring or damage the bowl. Be especially careful when installing stainless steel kitchen sinks, that the screws do not dimple the sink top. For a leak-free installation lay a thin bead of plumber's putty around the top of the bowl where the trim ring will compress it into a watertight gasket. The excess that oozes out can be cleaned up later with a toothpick without scratching the bowl.

FAUCET

The new faucet must match the spacing of openings in the bowl. Practically all lavatory faucets use 4-inch openings, i.e., ones spaced 4

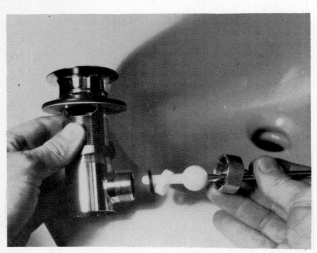

1. Before you install the lavatory pop-up drain parts, remove the pop-up lever and fittings from the lower half of the drain. Then unscrew the lower and upper halves and insert in the bowl.

2. Install the pop-up drain in the lavatory bowl using plumber's putty under the upper half. Next screw the tailpiece into the lower half of the drain, as tight as it will go by hand-turning.

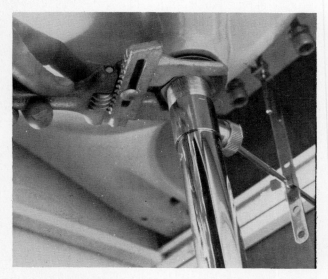

3. Assemble pop-up drain parts and tighten the drain into the bowl using a fixture-trap wrench, as shown, or a monkey wrench. The pop-rods can be adjusted for the desired height and action.

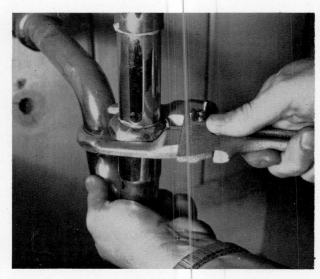

4. Use the wrench to tighten all trap slipnuts. Then you can run water into the lavatory and drain it to look for leaks. If you find any, tighten the slip-nuts securely until the leaks stop.

inches apart on centers. Most kitchen sinks, either three-hole or four-hole, are made to take faucets with 8-inch centers. Two- and three-hole sink bowls are standard for sinks without spray attachments. Four-hole sink bowls are intended for use with faucets having spray attachments. If you combine a four-holer and a faucet without sprayer, you will need a chrome plug snapped in to cover the exposed fourth hole. Put plumber's putty around it and install it in the right-hand opening.

Faucets on modern sinks are designed for deck-mounting. Some require the use of plumber's putty between the faucet body and the deck; others come with a rubber gasket that takes the place of putty. In any case, follow the directions with the faucet unit.

TRAP CONNECTION

Don't turn on the water until you have installed the drain system. Plumber's putty is used between the drain and the bowl to prevent leaking. Tighten the large ring nuts beneath each basket drain with a trap wrench or by pushing on the lugs with a screwdriver. Hold the drain so it does not turn with the nut.

Screw the short chromed tailpiece into the bottom of the lavatory drain. Put putty around the threads to prevent leaks. Fasten a rubber ring gasket, tailpiece, and slipnut to the lower end of each sink basket drain. The gasket goes between the tailpiece and the drain.

Put a slipnut over the tailpiece facing down, slip on a rubber gasket and install the first trap section loosely to the slipnut. Install the horizontal trap arm to the vertical one with a gasket

between and a slipnut to draw the connection tight. The trap arm slips into the waste pipe in the wall. (A floor hookup is slightly different, using an S-trap. Some codes do not permit S-traps.) Be sure to put a rubber gasket and slipnut over the trap arm before inserting it in the pipe. Align all the trap parts so they slope toward the waste pipe, then tighten all slipnuts without disturbing the alignment. Use a monkey wrench or a pipe wrench with adhesive bandages over its serrated jaws to protect the soft brass slipnuts. Turn on the fixture shutoff valves and watch the supply pipe for leaks.

Activated charcoal filter removes sediment and bad taste from drinking water. It usually mounts beneath the fixture in the cold-water line. Element is easily replaced when entirely used up.

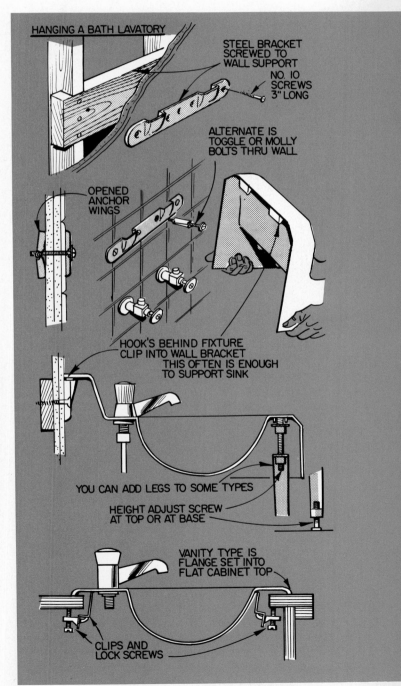

HANGING A BATH LAVATORY

STEEL BRACKET SCREWED TO WALL SUPPORT

NO. 10 SCREWS 3" LONG

ALTERNATE IS TOGGLE OR MOLLY BOLTS THRU WALL

OPENED ANCHOR WINGS

HOOK'S BEHIND FIXTURE CLIP INTO WALL BRACKET THIS OFTEN IS ENOUGH TO SUPPORT SINK

YOU CAN ADD LEGS TO SOME TYPES

HEIGHT ADJUST SCREW AT TOP OR AT BASE

VANITY TYPE IS FLANGE SET INTO FLAT CABINET TOP

CLIPS AND LOCK SCREWS

Changing a Toilet

A "john" is really not a permanent fixture. If yours is noisy, slow and hard to clean, turn it in for a new model.

The newer water closets have many features worthy of consideration. They are styled better and work more efficiently. You can install a new one in an hour!

MODERNIZING THE BATHROOM sooner or later calls for adding a modern toilet. Many low-cost houses have been built with low-cost washdown-type toilets. These use lots of water, are noisy, and provide only a minimum of bowl-protecting fill water. They are also frequently subject to clogging because their action is so sluggish. You can tell this type of toilet because its outlet is at the front of the bowl.

The replacement toilet you get can be one of the new, long single-piece tank-bowl models or a two-piece unit. Both will flush better and quieter than a washdown, and with less water.

We recommend getting either a siphon-jet or a siphon-vortex unit. While they cost more, they work so much better that they are worth the difference. In the siphon-jet, a built-in jet of water starts the flushing action as soon as the trip lever is depressed. The siphon-vortex gets the action going with a tornado-like whirlpool. The very least toilet you should get is a reverse-trap type. While this lacks an improved flushing action, it offers a large bowl seal and comes in modern elongated bowl design.

One thing to watch when buying a new toilet is to make certain the new unit's *rough in* dimension—the distance from the wall back of the tank to the center of the outlet horn on the bottom—matches the rough-in of your existing toilet. If it does not, you will have to make the toilet's waste pipe shorter or longer to suit. This doubles the work. Fortunately, practically all toilets use a 12-inch rough-in.

To check yours, measure from side bolts at the rear of the toilet base back to the wall. That distance is the toilet's rough-in, and it should be 12 inches. If it is more, a 12-inch rough-in toilet can still be used, however, it will leave a space between the toilet tank and the wall. If it is less, you will have to extend the toilet waste pipe out to center it 12 inches from the wall or else find a special toilet having the shorter rough-in.

REMOVAL

To get the old toilet out, first turn off the water. If it does not have a shutoff valve at the

A water closet is best located about two feet from your stack, so changing the location may be hard. But if you must (and your code permits), try the plastic bends. They're easy to install.

Special brass hold down bolts come in a few lengths to accommodate a marble slab under the fixture if you do not have a tile floor. Slip them in place in the flange slot. Keep vertical.

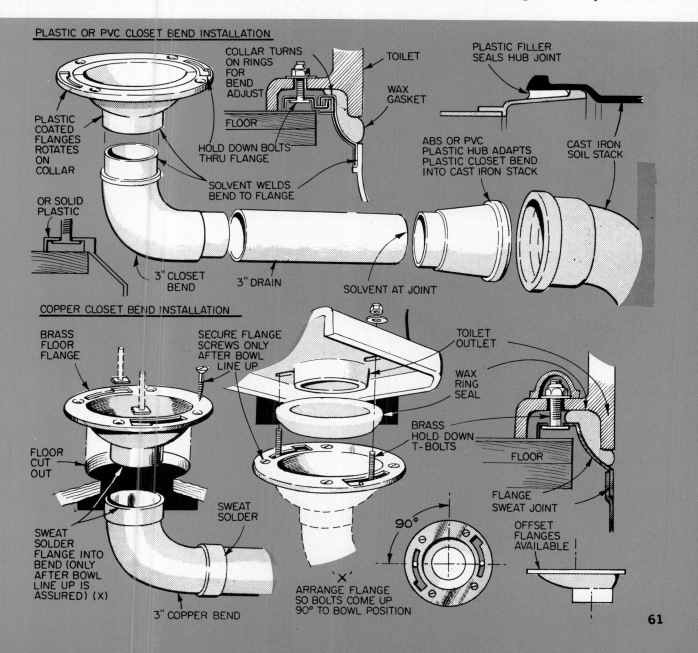

PLASTIC OR PVC CLOSET BEND INSTALLATION

COLLAR TURNS ON RINGS FOR BEND ADJUST

TOILET

WAX GASKET

FLOOR

PLASTIC COATED FLANGES ROTATES ON COLLAR

HOLD DOWN BOLTS THRU FLANGE

SOLVENT WELDS BEND TO FLANGE

PLASTIC FILLER SEALS HUB JOINT

ABS OR PVC PLASTIC HUB ADAPTS PLASTIC CLOSET BEND INTO CAST IRON STACK

CAST IRON SOIL STACK

OR SOLID PLASTIC

3" CLOSET BEND

3" DRAIN

SOLVENT AT JOINT

COPPER CLOSET BEND INSTALLATION

BRASS FLOOR FLANGE

SECURE FLANGE SCREWS ONLY AFTER BOWL LINE UP

TOILET OUTLET

WAX RING SEAL

BRASS HOLD DOWN T-BOLTS

FLOOR

FLOOR CUT OUT

SWEAT SOLDER

FLANGE SWEAT JOINT

SWEAT SOLDER FLANGE INTO BEND (ONLY AFTER BOWL LINE UP IS ASSURED) (X)

90°

'X' ARRANGE FLANGE SO BOLTS COME UP 90° TO BOWL POSITION

OFFSET FLANGES AVAILABLE

3" COPPER BEND

In renovation or new construction, it's always a good idea to cover the waste hole to prevent tools and debris from falling in. This plastic bend has a knock-out cover that is knocked out last.

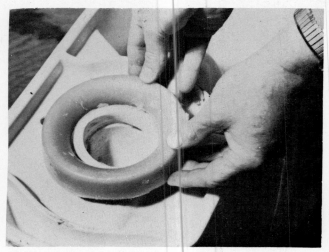

Inserting the wax seal on the fixture horn and making certain it will form an airtight seal is the most important part of installing a bowl. All seals are the same size and fit all horns.

Once your fixture is bolted to the floor, all you need do is connect the water supply. The new flexible copper (chrome-plated) supply tubes are cut to the exact length, then secured.

wall or floor, consider installing one as part of your changeover. An angle-stop or straight-stop valve screwed onto the pipe stub-out will enable easy shutoff when needed in the future.

Flush the toilet, holding the trip handle de-

pressed until most of the water drains out of the tank. Get rid of the rest of the tank water by sopping it up with a sponge. Disconnect the supply pipe underneath the left side of the toilet tank. Removal of the flange nut from the ball cock valve base will do the job.

Take the two tank-to-bowl bolts out from inside the tank. If they are badly corroded, you may have to hold them with locking pliers while you apply enough force to break them. Now the tank can be lifted from the toilet bowl. If the tank is wall-mounted, disconnect the flush pipe between it and the bowl and lift it off its wall bracket and remove the bracket, too.

To get the toilet bowl out, pry the covers from the base bolts, and remove the nuts thus exposed. Stand straddling the bowl, twist it, rock it, and lift. This should break the seal with the floor flange and let the bowl be lifted free. Be careful not to tilt it backward or some bowl water may come out the discharge opening.

Now scrape out any putty or wax left in the closet flange cavity, leaving it clean. Install two new flange bolts in the slots of the closet flange, holding them vertical with plumber's putty.

Unpack the new toilet carefully and read the instruction sheet. Follow the specific directions given for the installation. In general, it goes like this:

Invert the bowl on newspapers to prevent scratching and lay a ring of plumber's putty around the base flange. Slip a new wax toilet gasket down over the outlet horn on the bottom of the toilet bowl. Pick up the toilet, invert it,

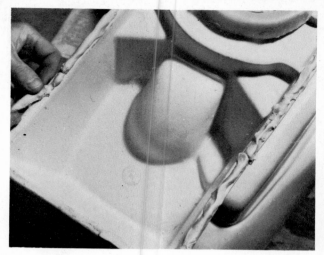

In addition to bolts holding the fixture, pack a bead of plumber's putty around the rim to fill in any uneven spots in the floor. With tile floors you can set the bowl in a bed of plaster.

One of the most difficult jobs is to thread the bowl on the flange hold-down bolts and have the wax seal set perfectly around the opening. Press down firmly until both the wax and putty settles.

and carry it over to the closet flange. Lower it gently and squarely, mating the outlet horn with the closet flange and getting the two bolts through the holes provided in the toilet base. Press down and rock the bowl gently to compress the wax gasket into the closet flange. This should bring the bowl square with the back wall and level on the floor. Install the base nuts over washers and tighten them snugly but gently. Scrape up excess putty squeezed out from the base. The base nuts are intended to be covered with plastic or ceramic caps. Stuff some putty inside the caps and stick them on over the bolts. Scrape up the excess.

TANK INSTALLATION

Two-piece tank/bowl toilets come with the parts separated for easier handling. Set the tank over the bowl's water inlet, using the rubber gasket supplied. Install the bolts and their gaskets, tightening them snugly. Make sure that the tank is aligned with the wall.

Connect the water-supply tube, put on the tank top and install a new toilet seat. The toilet seat hardware fits through two holes in the top of the toilet bowl. Modern elongated bowls need elongated toilet seats. Use the rubber washers against the bowl to protect it from damage when the nuts are tightened. Get them tight enough to hold the seat in proper alignment but not so tight that they might crack the bowl.

Turn on the water and check your installation for leaks during filling and flushing.

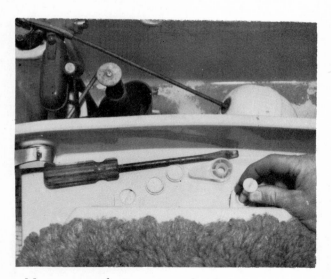

Most manufacturers supply their own seats, which are bolted in place. Bolts are either plastic or brass. Some of the new fixtures have seats with a catch for quick removal and easy cleaning.

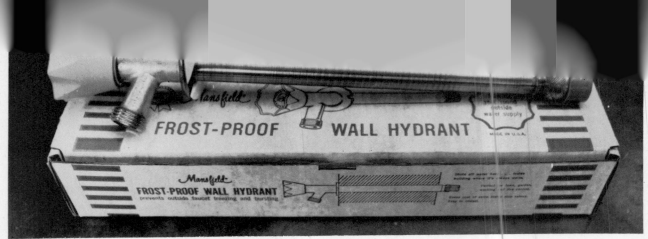

A freezeproof hydrant-type faucet is the best solution to providing an add-on hose bib for your house. While the faucet outlet is outdoors in the cold, water is shut off inside the house. Available in ½″ and ¾″.

Add an Outside Hose Outlet

Outside hose outlets should be planned before you build, but if you need one or two extra spigots now they are easy to install.

If your house was shorted on outdoor garden hose spigots, you can add more. It involves tapping onto the house cold-water main ahead of the water softener and water heater—but not ahead of the water meter—and running pipes to the desired outdoor locations.

Before you get the materials, choose a pipe route from the cold-water main to the through-wall location heading outdoors. The cold-water tap-off may be made easiest with a saddle tee, although this restricts water flow considerably. If you want full flow, say for a sprinkler or for car-washing, you will have to install a tee in the cold-water main. Pipe ends that are cut off must be rethreaded and a union installed to let you do the necessary thread makeup. The slip-nut tee can be inserted between the cut pipes without rethreading. Copper and plastic systems, once drained of water, will accept a new tee easily by pushing the pipes back enough to fit. The run of any installed tee should be sized to fit the cold-water main which is often ¾-inch. The tapped opening should be ½-inch, the recommended size of the new pipe run.

From there, ½-inch elbows, couplings, and pipe should take you the rest of the way.

At the spigot end of the run install a fitting for the hose bibb. These can be had with male or female threads that screw right onto the pipe.

If you live in a freezing climate, you will want to use a freeze-proof through-wall outdoor hydrant. These require a horizontal installation. They shut off the water inside the wall.

If your code permits, PVC plastic pipe is recommended for the entire installation. Use a ½-inch male adapter at the slipnut coupling or tapping tee and solvent-weld the first run of pipe to it. Go from there with solvent-welded plastic pipe and fittings. At the spigot end install another ½-inch male or female adapter and screw on the faucet. If the freeze-proof hydrant you use has ¾-inch male threads, simply end the pipe run with a ½ x ¾-inch bushing and a ¾-inch female adapter. Solvent-weld them to the plastic pipe.

Framing members that are in the way can be drilled with a 1-inch wood boring bit chucked in a ¼-inch electric drill. Same with drilling through a clapboard wall. Drill between studs, not through them. If masonry must be drilled use a carbide-tipped masonry bit in your drill and, if you can, go through in soft mortar joints. In any case, the hole through the wall should be in a straight line so that the pipes will fit. The faucet you use should have a flange big enough to cover the hole. Turn on the water and flush the new pipe before closing the faucet. Check the entire run for leaks.

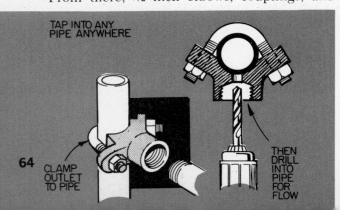

TAP INTO ANY PIPE ANYWHERE

CLAMP OUTLET TO PIPE

THEN DRILL INTO PIPE FOR FLOW

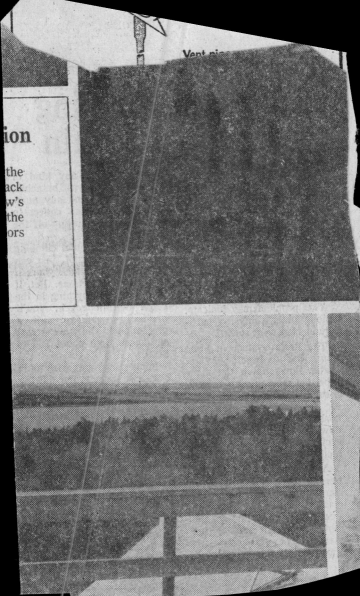

Vent p...

ion

the
ack
w's
the
ors

Vacation retreat shows imaginat

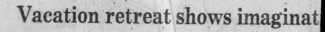

FIREPLACE, above, dominates the living room of
Thomas Todd vacation home in Jamestown. Tr:
lighting can be seen on the walls. Below, the cro
nest gives a view of the Bay. Below right is
dining area as seen from the living room. The fl
are oak.

PICTURES BY LAWRENCE S. MILLARD

Three ways to tap into a cold-water main: left, a slip-coupling tee for galvanized steel pipe works without threading. Others are saddle tees, which restrict the water flow. A slip-coupling is best.

1. To run a new water line from the cold-water main, first shut off water at the house main. Then installed a tapping tee with its rubber gasket against the pipe. Tighten securely to pipe.

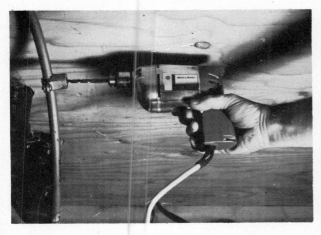

2. Next drill an opening into the pipe through the tap tee. Directions with it specify the drill size to use. The tee is ordered to fit the size and type of water pipe. All sizes are available.

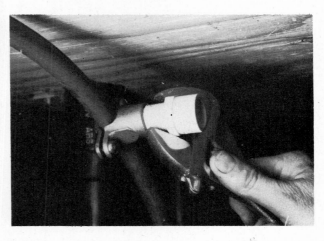

3. Tighten a plastic-to-threads adapter into the saddle tee, first coating its threads with thread-seal compound designed for plastic fittings. Now you're ready to make new run with PVC pipe.

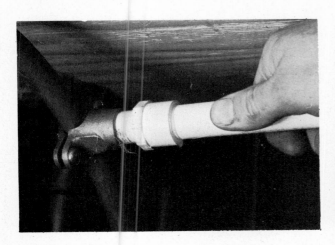

4. Solvent-weld the first length of PVC plastic pipe to the adapter, as described in a previous chapter. Drill out framing where necessary to pass the pipe. Hang it so pipe can slide a bit.

5. Finish the installation to an outside wall with a plastic-to-threads adapter. Final step is to screw the hose bib or freeze-proof hydrant onto adapter. Hold it from turning with a wrench.

Changing Faucets

If your sink is readily accessible you can easily replace any faucet. And you'll save anywhere from $15 to $25 and up if you do it yourself.

Sink faucets are usually 8' on centers. This four-hole Carrollton stainless steel double-bowl sink takes Peerless single-lever self-sealing faucet with spray attachment using all four of the holes.

FAUCETS SOMETIMES reach the point where they cannot be successfully repaired. These oldies are more trouble than they are worth. You can easily replace them. Today's faucets, especially the better ones, are designed to last for years without problems.

Faucet replacement begins with selection of the new unit. Whether it is for sink, lavatory or laundry, you have to decide whether you want separate faucets or a single-unit mixing faucet.

Then you must decide how good a faucet to get, in quality and in appearance. Quality in function mostly pays for itself in longer life and less trouble. A $25 faucet unit should outlast two $12 ones. What's more, it will look better.

Another decision in selecting a lavatory faucet is whether you want one with a pop-up drain. Chances are if the old unit had a pop-up drain, you'll want to retain that feature.

Order a mixing faucet to match the bowl's hole centers: 4-inch centers for lavatories (nearly all) and usually 8-inch centers for sink and built-in laundry tub faucets.

TAKE-APART

On a lavatory, start with the drain. Using a trap wrench, or monkey wrench, loosen all the slipnuts. Take apart the old pop-up drain parts, removing the pop-lever from the drain. Unscrew the tailpiece from the drain, if it will come, otherwise leave it. Remove the drain plug. Sometimes a counterclockwise twist is needed to get it free.

FAUCET REMOVAL

To take off the old faucet, turn off the water to the fixture. Plan on replacing the supply tubes, too. When you remove the upper end of the supply tubes, you will probably need a tool called a basin wrench. Room to work is limited behind the bowl and this tool is the only prac-

If your new kitchen or lavatory faucet unit you buy doesn't come with a built-in rubber gasket for the escutcheon, install a ring of plumber's putty under the escutcheon as a seal. Trim excess.

Any adapters that can be installed on a faucet's water-supply tubes before inserting it into the fixture should be installed and tightened. It's much tougher to do once the faucet is in place.

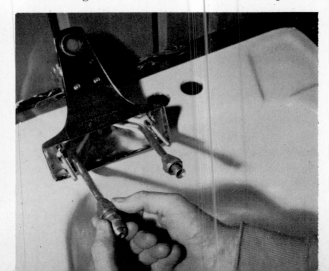

tical way of turning the flange nuts. It also works on the fixture hold-down nuts, which must be taken off too. Set the serrated basin wrench grabber bar one way to remove, the other way later to tighten. A basin wrench costs little and makes a lifetime addition to your plumbing tools.

With the water supply tubes disconnected and the hold-down nuts off, the old faucet can be lifted out of the bowl.

INSTALLING THE NEW

Unpack the new faucet unit and follow the specific directions prepared by the manufacturer. Here are a few points we would like to add. Faucets without built-in gaskets should be installed on a ring of plumber's putty. Lay the putty out of the bowl-top and lower the faucet in place. Install the hold-down nuts over the faucet stubs below the bowl, being sure to use the washers provided.

You will find so many combinations of water-supply outlets and faucet requirements that your home center or hardware dealer should be consulted on the method of bringing water from the wall or floor to the faucet. In any case, you will find a good assortment of fixture supply pipe and the fittings for each end available. Most houses today have angle-stop valves at the wall for both hot and cold water. These take the plain end of a 3/8-inch flexible chromed water supply tube directly through a ferrule and compression nut. This end is cut off so that the upper end of the supply tube can reach the faucet tailpiece and connect to it. Normally the tailpiece connection is made with a rubber washer and a flange nut which should be purchased separately.

Some faucets have no threaded fitting on the end of the tailpiece, just a plain tubing end. This hookup can be made with a flare or compression fitting. Consult your dealer for the parts.

Hook in the pop-up drain parts in the opposite way described for taking them out. But remember to put plumber's putty between the upper drain and the bowl, and use the furnished rubber washer between the lower one and the bowl. Connect the trap and drain-control lever to the control rod and adjust it for free action.

Remove the faucet aerator. Turn on both hot and cold water and let them run for a minute to clear any debris from the pipes. Install the aerator and run in a bowl-full of water. Drain the bowl and check for leaks in the trap system. Leaks are usually stopped by further tightening of nuts.

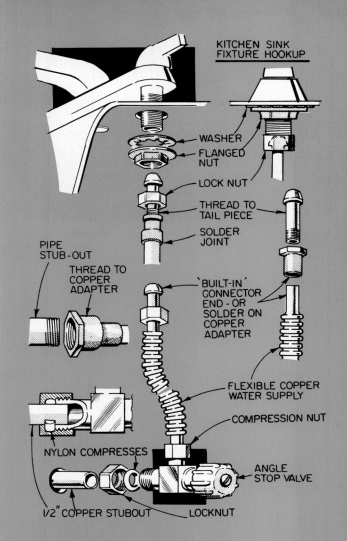

KITCHEN SINK FIXTURE HOOKUP

WASHER
FLANGED NUT
LOCK NUT
THREAD TO TAIL PIECE
SOLDER JOINT
PIPE STUB-OUT
THREAD TO COPPER ADAPTER
'BUILT-IN' CONNECTOR END - OR SOLDER ON COPPER ADAPTER
FLEXIBLE COPPER WATER SUPPLY
COMPRESSION NUT
NYLON COMPRESSES
1/2" COPPER STUBOUT
LOCKNUT
ANGLE STOP VALVE

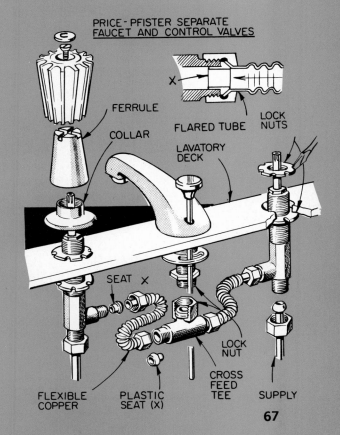

PRICE - PFISTER SEPARATE FAUCET AND CONTROL VALVES

FERRULE
COLLAR
X
FLARED TUBE
LOCK NUTS
LAVATORY DECK
SEAT X
LOCK NUT
FLEXIBLE COPPER
PLASTIC SEAT (X)
CROSS FEED TEE
SUPPLY

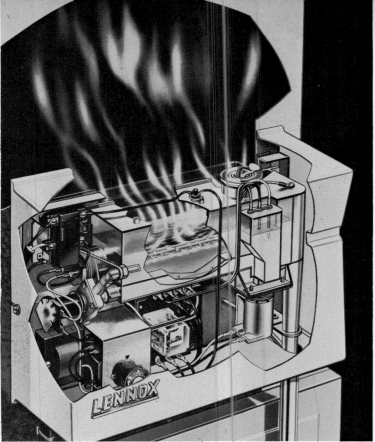

A power humidifier mounts to the furnace hot-air plenum and literally pumps water into the air. A humidified house is more comfortable, even at cooler temperatures, and more healthful.

Proper humidity is usually never a problem with steam or hot water heating systems, but with warm air it can be. So

Install a Humidifier

HEATED AIR IS DRY AIR. Outside winter air at 20° and a relative humidity of 40 per cent brought into your home and heated to room temperature becomes an uncomfortably dry 6 per cent relative humidity. Relative humidity should be 35 to 40 per cent to be comfortable. With proper humidification you can set the thermostat lower and still feel comfortable.

The only way to get proper humidity is to install a power humidifier to "pump" water into the air. If you have a warm-air heating system, you can do it. The low-cost plate-type units will not do the job. Some of these come with furnaces and they help a little, but not very much.

HUMIDISTAT

The best power humidifiers come with wall-mounted humidistats to make humidity control as easy as temperature control. Set it and forget it. Homes heated by hot water or steam must use costlier room-type power humidifiers. No installation is required. Just plug in and keep filled with water.

With adequate house humidity, your family will probably have far fewer colds. My family has seen this added benefit of power humidification. There are other benefits, too.

If your water supply contains minerals, the power unit you get should be one of the self-cleaning types. Softening the water will not remove minerals; it merely changes them to a form more compatible for household use. They will still cause heavy lime scale in a humidifier. Do not use the humidifiers that spray water into the air, for these also spray water-borne minerals into your air. There they soon settle out on furniture and all over the house. The only way you can use one of these in a hard-water area is to pipe water to it through what's called a demineralizer. It creates water that is free of impurities.

INSTALLATION TIPS

Installation is easy, following instructions with the unit you buy. Start by cutting an opening in the furnace hot-air plenum using metal snips. Drill out the humidifier mounting holes. Mount the plenum-stiffener (if used), then the humidifier body. Caulk the mounting holes, if required, using non-hardening polybutene rope caulk.

Run a ¼-inch water line from the nearest cold-water pipe using a saddle valve tap-in. Flexible copper or vinyl tubing and compression fittings make it easy. If an overflow tube on the humidifier is required by your code,

POWER HUMIDIFIER-PLENUM MOUNTED

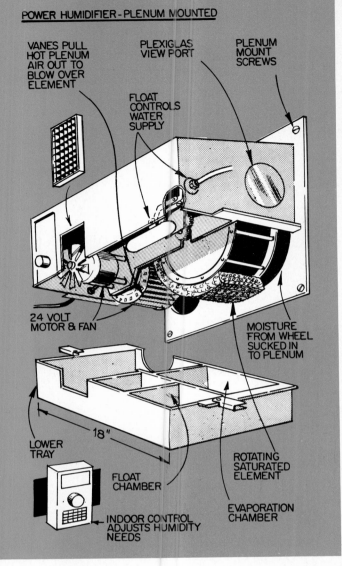

VANES PULL HOT PLENUM AIR OUT TO BLOW OVER ELEMENT

PLEXIGLAS VIEW PORT

PLENUM MOUNT SCREWS

FLOAT CONTROLS WATER SUPPLY

24 VOLT MOTOR & FAN

MOISTURE FROM WHEEL SUCKED IN TO PLENUM

LOWER TRAY

18"

FLOAT CHAMBER

ROTATING SATURATED ELEMENT

EVAPORATION CHAMBER

INDOOR CONTROL ADJUSTS HUMIDITY NEEDS

The new solid state humidistats will insure the desired relative humidity at all times. Humidifiers are usually necessary in the winter time; they are cleaned and turned off in the summer.

punch out the opening and install it. Run the overflow pipe to a good drain point where the water can run away.

Make 120-volt power connections as detailed with the unit. If a humidistat is used, its low-voltage wiring may usually be stapled right to the house framing.

Turn on the saddle valve and the electric power and test your unit. It should run only when the furnace blower is operating. The humidifier may also be mounted in a large main air duct or away from the furnace and ducted to it. The instruction sheet should detail just how it is done.

Your power humidifier probably comes in a kit like this Sears product which includes the unit, a solid-state humidistat, mounting hardware and the necessary tubing to complete the hookup.

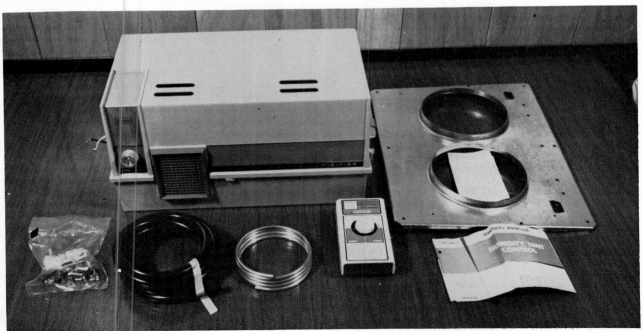

Washing Machine Plumbing

The installation of a normal washing machine requires very little plumbing. All you need is access to a hot and cold water line plus a nearby drain.

Hot and cold water shut-off valves should be readily accessible in case you wish to move the machine or else the rubber hoses break. The Duo-cloz valve shown on page 71 is preferable.

Besides the plumbing connections described in the text, a washer-dryer setup needs an electrical box installed nearby, plus an outside vent for a gas dryer. Install these while the wall's open.

YOU CAN HAVE the convenience of an upstairs laundry with automatic washer by putting in the necessary drain and water-supply pipes. Running the supply pipes is much the same as adding an outdoor hose outlet. The difference is that both hot-water and cold-water lines are run parallel to each other but at least 6 inches apart. The hot is brought up on the left side of the washer and the cold is brought up on the right side. Air chambers, capped 12-inch lengths of pipe, should rise above the hose faucets. This can be done by using tees in the lines at the faucets. Use ½-inch CPVC plastic pipe for the easiest working, and saddle tapping tees or slip-nut tees at the water mains. Both tee-offs should be located after the water softener has done its thing.

CLOSE TO STACK

For the easiest job, locate the washer within a few feet of any vent stack. This lets you avoid installing new vent runs for the washer drain. The 1½-inch diameter washer waste pipe may run 3½ feet total horizontal length to the point where it enters the vent stack. Okay by National Plumbing Code. If the run is longer, you may have to use a large waste pipe or provide separate venting. (A 2-inch pipe may run 5 feet.) Instead of draining into a vent stack, you may connect into the main building drain. Then, no matter how short the run, separate venting must always be provided for the washer drain.

DRAIN CONNECTIONS

Start at the vent stack or building drain. Cut out enough of it to let you install a tee-wye fitting below the floor, aimed in the direction of the flow. If your DWV house system is plastic and code permits, you can cut a hole in the vent stack and install a solvent-welded saddle

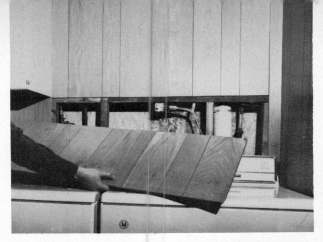

The finished installation looks as though it belongs. Done this way, no pipes need show outside the wall. Drains and water supply pipes all connect up or go down behind the finished wall.

Prefinished plywood hardwood paneling covers the wall framing and utilities to a washer-dryer combo. Installed with small screws, an access panel designed so that you can remove if needed.

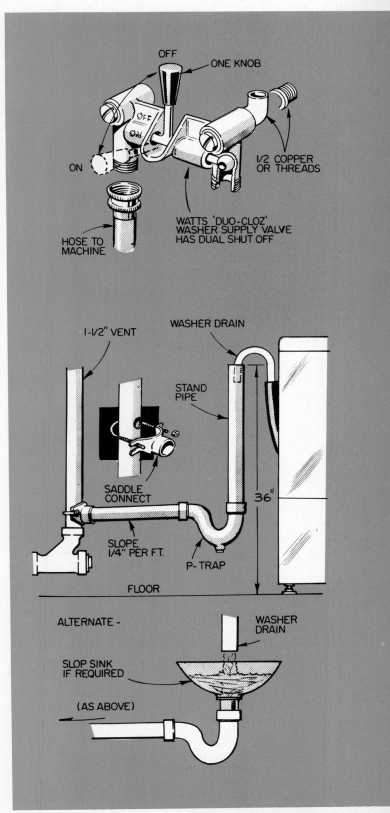

tee over it. Wire it temporarily to hold while the solvent sets. On a cast iron system, use a 3 x 3 x 1½ inch No-Hub tee wye. On a copper or plastic system you can install a 3 x 3 x 1½-inch tee-wye in the cut 3-inch vent. Aim the tee centered on the point where the washer drain will pass through the floor. Run the pipe, sloping it up and away from the stack ¼ inch per foot. Install a P-trap so that it faces upward through a hole in the floor behind the washer. These are available in plastic, copper and threaded steel in the 1½-inch size. They make the right-angle bend without other fittings. If the horizontal distance is more than the maximum wet-vent distance, a cleanout should be provided. Use a 1½-inch tee-wye fitting at the outlet end of the P-trap, with a removable plug in the branch end. Up from the trap extends the 1½-inch vertical washer standpipe. Cut it off about 36 inches above the floor. Slip in the washer drain hose and you are ready to wash.

Here's one way to raise the roof and add on to your living space. In this case the exterior walls were finished and made weather tight. Then the stacks were extended and rooms partitioned.

Plumbing Tips for an Add-on Room

Solving plumbing problems is a lot easier than solving structural problems. Here are some answers to your questions.

PLUMBING FOR AN EXTRA bathroom involves a lot more than merely adding a washing machine drain, as in the previous chapter. You should understand all the basics covered in the first chapter before tackling an extra bathroom. Then study the drawings. Don't tackle this major add-on work unless you understand what you're doing. Millions of homeowners have done their own work. You probably can too. But be informed—and confident—before you begin.

The project involves tapping into the existing hot and cold-water mains and extending them to the new bathroom. From there the pipes must be carried to each toilet, lavatory and tub or shower. The pipes are small and may go up or down as needed, so this is easy. Much toucher is finding a route for the add-on 3-inch drain line to handle waste water, and perhaps running a new vent stack up through the roof to provide necessary venting for the new fixture traps.

The first step is to draw a plan. It needn't be fancy, just a sketch showing what's already there and what you plan to add. Then plan how you'll run the DWV pipes. Walls will have to be opened up. Floors, ceilings, and roof will have to be drilled to provide a passage for the new stack.

If you're lucky enough to have an existing 3- or 4-inch vent stack in one wall of the added bath, it could be tapped to save putting in the new stack. A new stack may be easier to install. Whatever stack is used must be at least 3 inches in diameter to serve a toilet. The toilet should be located as close as possible to the vent stack. Seldom is more than 16 inches separation permitted.

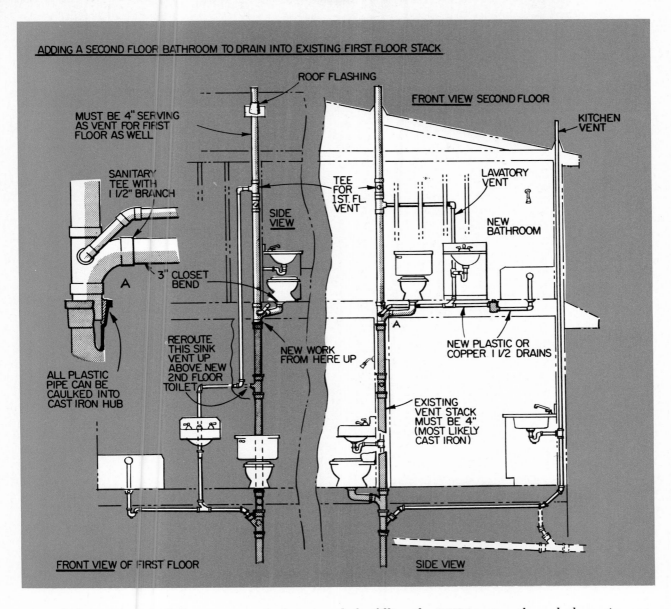

ROOF FLASHING

MUST BE 4" SERVING AS VENT FOR FIRST FLOOR AS WELL

SANITARY TEE WITH 1 1/2" BRANCH

3" CLOSET BEND

A

ALL PLASTIC PIPE CAN BE CAULKED INTO CAST IRON HUB

SIDE VIEW

TEE FOR 1ST. FL VENT

FRONT VIEW SECOND FLOOR

KITCHEN VENT

LAVATORY VENT

NEW BATHROOM

REROUTE THIS SINK VENT UP ABOVE NEW 2ND FLOOR TOILET

NEW WORK FROM HERE UP

NEW PLASTIC OR COPPER 1 1/2 DRAINS

A

EXISTING VENT STACK MUST BE 4" (MOST LIKELY CAST IRON)

FRONT VIEW OF FIRST FLOOR

SIDE VIEW

Proof of your work is drain-waste-vent leak-test made by filling the DWV system through the main vent stack above the roof. Then inspect every joint of system for water leaks immediately and also 4 hours later.

When adding a new stack, always cut through the roof after the inside pipe is in place and you can transfer the measurement. Cut a small hole, peek down at the pipe and then enlarge the hole.

WET-VENTS

Other fixtures should be located so their waste pipes can run to the stack without need for reventing. Wet-vent distances (maximum) allowed by the National Plumbing Code are as follows:

> 1½-inch pipe—3½ feet
> 2-inch pipe—5 feet
> 3-inch pipe—6 feet
> 4-inch pipe—10 feet

If this proves impractical, one fixture can be placed across the room where it is revented. Its drain, thus, would run down from the fixture, then across and into the vent stack. Its vent would run up from the fixture across the ceiling and join the vent stack above where the highest fixture drains.

A drainage tee in the wall behind the fixture

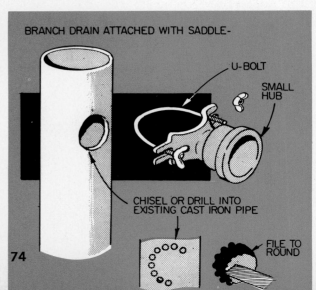

BRANCH DRAIN ATTACHED WITH SADDLE-

U-BOLT

SMALL HUB

CHISEL OR DRILL INTO EXISTING CAST IRON PIPE

FILE TO ROUND

74

Horizontal runs of DWV piping should slope about ¼″ per foot. The fittings, if properly installed, are designed to set up the right slope; drain runs slope toward stack, vent slopes away.

is placed with its smooth curved passage going down to act as starter for both drain and vent. A stub-out enters the room and later the trap is connected to it.

Next give some thought to routing of water-supply pipes, especially the hot-water line. Hot piping runs from the water heater should be kept short and direct. All runs should contain as few elbows and bends as possible. The whole new bath can be served by ½-inch hot and cold water-water pipes. They should connect to the existing mains with full-flow fittings, not with restricting saddle tees.

Finally, consider how the new room's drain pipe will reach the existing house drain or sewer. The easiest method is to connect outdoors underground to the existing sewer or septic tank line. Some codes won't permit this. An indoor hookup depends on how close the add-on room is to the existing building drain. Re-

Common Pipe Sizes		
Purpose	Water Supply	DWV
Main	¾″	3″
Room Branches	½″	2″
Soil Stack (Main)	—	3″
Vent Stack (no Toilet)	—	1½″
House Sewer	—	4″
Septic Systems	—	4″
House Main	1″	—
Toilets	½″	3″
Sinks, laundry tubs	½″	1½″
Lavatories	½″	1½″°
Bathtubs	½″	1½″
Showers	½″	2″
Hose spigots	½″	—
Humidifiers, coolers	¼″	—

Silicone compounds are available in a wide range of colors to make a watertight tub and wall joint. Unlike regular grout, the material is flexible and stretches as the house settles.

The no-mess way to use this material is to stick masking a tape about ¼″ from both the wall and the tub. Then cut the nozzle to the correct width and squeeze a bead. Pull tape off.

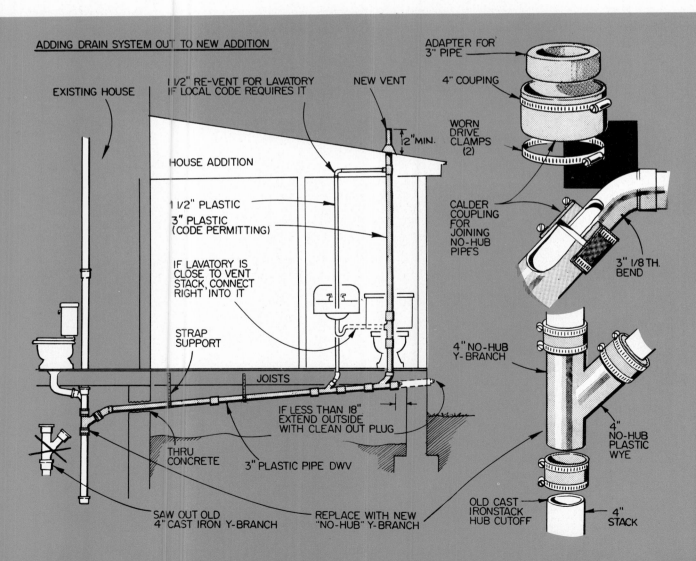

ADDING DRAIN SYSTEM OUT TO NEW ADDITION

EXISTING HOUSE

1 1/2" RE-VENT FOR LAVATORY IF LOCAL CODE REQUIRES IT

NEW VENT

2"MIN.

HOUSE ADDITION

1 1/2" PLASTIC

3" PLASTIC (CODE PERMITTING)

IF LAVATORY IS CLOSE TO VENT STACK, CONNECT RIGHT INTO IT

STRAP SUPPORT

JOISTS

IF LESS THAN 18" EXTEND OUTSIDE WITH CLEAN OUT PLUG

THRU CONCRETE

3" PLASTIC PIPE DWV

SAW OUT OLD 4" CAST IRON Y-BRANCH

REPLACE WITH NEW "NO-HUB" Y-BRANCH

ADAPTER FOR 3" PIPE

4" COUPING

WORN DRIVE CLAMPS (2)

CALDER COUPLING FOR JOINING NO-HUB PIPES

3" 1/8TH. BEND

4" NO-HUB Y-BRANCH

4" NO-HUB PLASTIC WYE

OLD CAST IRONSTACK HUB CUTOFF

4" STACK

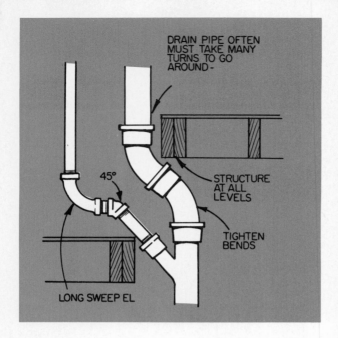

DRAIN PIPE OFTEN MUST TAKE MANY TURNS TO GO AROUND -

45°

LONG SWEEP EL

STRUCTURE AT ALL LEVELS

TIGHTEN BENDS

member that the new drain must slope ¼-inch per foot toward the drain. Install the sloped portion at proper pitch, then elbow straight down if it needs to go lower to reach the building drain. Avoid 90° bends in horizontal drain runs; use two 45° quarter bends instead.

Drains entering other drain pipes—except vertical ones—should do so at a 45° angle through tee-wyes instead of at right angles through tees. (Some codes say that drains may only enter a stack.) A drain emptying into a vertical pipe may do so at a right angle. However,

if there is space, the connection should be made at a 45° angle. Toilets should enter directly into the stack behind the toilet. Two toilets may be connected back to back on one vent stack by using a double sanitary tee fitting.

MORE RULES OF GOOD DWV WORK

Every horizontal drainage run (except short wet-vents that can be reached for cleaning through the fixture trap) should have a cleanout fitting installed at the higher end. The cleanout must be accessible inside or outside the house or in the basement or crawlspace. It should be no closer than 18 inches to a wall to allow room to get a cleanout tool into the pipe run. If it comes too close, the cleanout should be extended through the wall with pipe and the cleanout cover installed on the other side of the wall. Sometimes cleanouts are installed outside of buildings, so they'll be accessible. Most, however, can be reached through the basement or crawlspace.

All vent piping must connect to drain lines from the top. From there the vent must rise vertically at no less than a 45-degree angle until it is 6 inches higher than the flood rim of the fixture it serves. This keeps drain water from backing up in vent piping, possibly clogging it.

If there are fixtures on both stories of two-story construction and there is a toilet on the second story, all first-floor revents will probably have to tie into the vent stack above the highest fixture drain on the second floor. Usually this

When you build a stall shower, set the base in place and frame out the walls. Then connect the drain and hot and cold water lines to the faucet. We recommend one of the new single dial units.

Holes for new pipe runs are cut where needed in floors, ceilings, walls. Do it by drilling a series of holes or just saw them. A 3″ copper DWV vent pipe fits snugly within a 2 x 4 stud wall

means reventing them above the second-story ceiling.

Under some codes, sinks and lavatories may drain into a soil stack above the toilet. In others, these drain runs must be carried down through the floor and enter the soil stack below the toilet's entrance. Then reventing of each is necessary to prevent trap siphonage.

RUNNING PIPES

Start your installation at the toilet's sanitary tee. Put a large nail through the floor centered on the toilet and 12 inches out from the finished wall. Go below and check to see if any framing is in the way. If not, proceed. Open the wall behind the toilet and cut openings for the toilet's sanitary tee and soil stack. If you use a 3-inch copper, No-Hub cast iron, or PVC plastic DWV system, the wall need not be furred out. A 3-inch ABS system needs a 4½-inch wall. Use a 2 x 8 wall for a 4-inch leaded cast iron system. Start assembling the system with the sanitary tee behind the toilet. Its smoothly rounded slope should follow the direction the water will take. Install the toilet waste pipe, closet bend, and closet flange, cutting out for the closet flange around the large nail in the floor, on which it should be centered. Set the closet flange so its side slots are square with the rear wall.

Next, work up from the sanitary tee, installing a 3 x 3 x 1½ tee for the lavatory with its branch opening centered 16 inches above the finished floor and aimed to connect to the lavatory waste pipe. If revents are being used, be sure to incorporate tees for them as you go up. These are installed upside down, with the smooth curve heading upward. Finally, go out through the roof 6 inches above or more. A flashing should be worked under the shingles for a leak-free joint. Some codes call for a vent increaser through the roof, perhaps to 6 inches in diameter. Check.

Notches for piping should follow the notching rules. Now work down from the sanitary tee. Put in a 3 x 3 x 1½ tee for the bathtub drain or a 3 x 3 x 2 tee for a shower drain. If the lavatory drains below the toilet, put in a 3 x 3 x 1½ tee. Then turn the soil stack horizontally, providing a cleanout opening at the turn, and carry it to its connection with the building drain. A good place to make an easy connection to the building drain is at an existing cleanout.

Next install the various waste lines and their revents, if used. The bathtub or shower trap should be installed as a part of its waste line. The lavatory gets a separate trap, later. The toilet contains its own bowl trap.

WATER-SUPPLY LINES

Connecting water pipes to your add-on bath is much like adding washer supply pipes. Use 12-inch-long air chambers at every fixture except the toilet. Stub-out pipes entering the room from the wall should be ½-inch. Install temporary caps on them.

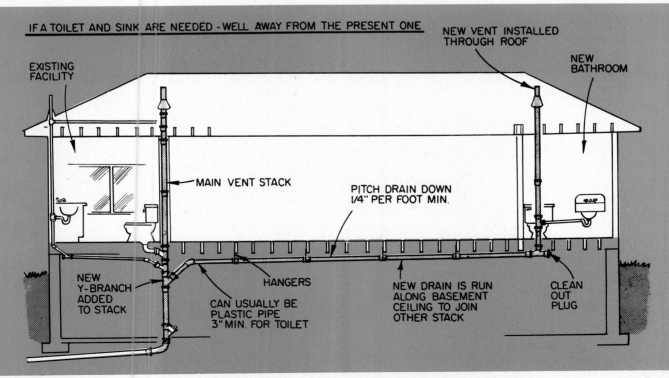

IF A TOILET AND SINK ARE NEEDED - WELL AWAY FROM THE PRESENT ONE

NEW VENT INSTALLED THROUGH ROOF

NEW BATHROOM

EXISTING FACILITY

MAIN VENT STACK

PITCH DRAIN DOWN 1/4" PER FOOT MIN.

NEW Y-BRANCH ADDED TO STACK

HANGERS

CAN USUALLY BE PLASTIC PIPE 3" MIN. FOR TOILET

NEW DRAIN IS RUN ALONG BASEMENT CEILING TO JOIN OTHER STACK

CLEAN OUT PLUG

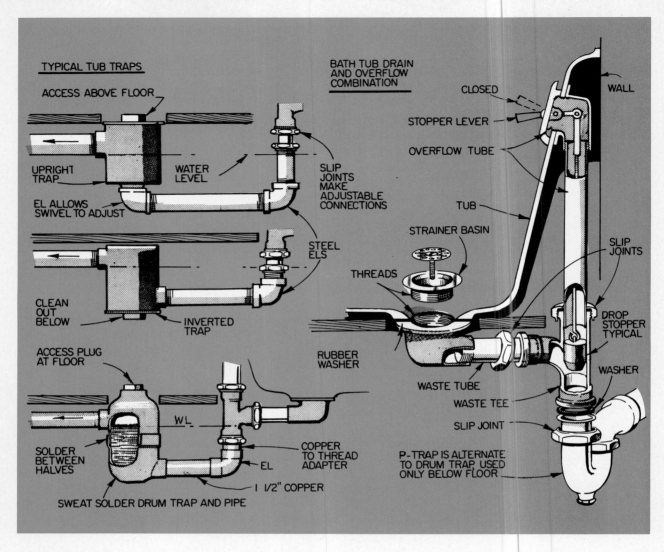

TYPICAL TUB TRAPS

ACCESS ABOVE FLOOR

UPRIGHT TRAP

WATER LEVEL

EL ALLOWS SWIVEL TO ADJUST

SLIP JOINTS MAKE ADJUSTABLE CONNECTIONS

CLEAN OUT BELOW

STEEL ELS

INVERTED TRAP

ACCESS PLUG AT FLOOR

RUBBER WASHER

W.L.

SOLDER BETWEEN HALVES

SWEAT SOLDER DRUM TRAP AND PIPE

EL

1 1/2" COPPER

COPPER TO THREAD ADAPTER

BATH TUB DRAIN AND OVERFLOW COMBINATION

CLOSED

WALL

STOPPER LEVER

OVERFLOW TUBE

TUB

STRAINER BASIN

SLIP JOINTS

THREADS

DROP STOPPER TYPICAL

WASHER

WASTE TUBE

WASTE TEE

SLIP JOINT

P-TRAP IS ALTERNATE TO DRUM TRAP USED ONLY BELOW FLOOR

The completed plumbing system should be water-tested and inspected before closing in the walls. Make sure everything is capped, then turn on the water and check for leaks immediately and after 4 hours. To test DWV piping, plug all fixture waste pipe openings. Ready-made solvent-welded plugs can be used in a plastic system. Later they're cut out. Otherwise, use concrete or mortar-packed plugs on top of newspapers. The lower end must likewise be plugged off from draining into the existing drain. Later, after the plugs have set, run water from a garden hose into the roof vent, filling the new DWV system with water. Check every joint for leakage. Leave the hose in but turned off. When the inspector comes, he'll turn on the water. If he sees an immediate cascade of water come from the roof vent, he knows there is no DWV leakage.

FIXTURES

Rough plumbing completed, you can close in the walls with whatever material you wish and install the fixtures. When installing a tub, you'll need to provide a 12 x 14-inch-wide access at the head end of the tub through the floor for installing the overflow and waste fittings to the trap. The use of front-access tub/shower faucet hardware eliminates the need for providing for access behind them. The large escutcheon gives all the room you need for servicing and replacement. The tub waste uses a slipnut connection, just like a lavatory but 1 1/2-inch, not 1 1/4-inch.

A shower consists of a watertight floor pan with a cabinet above. You can buy a readymade unit or make one. In any case, it's best to buy the floor pan. Install its drain fitting and lower it over the 2-inch waste riser coming up from the floor. The riser should be cut off below shower floor level. Calk the joint between the drain and waste pipe with oakum and lead. A shower control valve centered 48 inches high reaches through a hole cut in the shower cabinet. Set the shower head outlet at eye level or higher and install the chromed shower pipe, and head.

RULES FOR NOTCHING

(1) Notch joists only in their end quarters; never in the center half. Then notch no more one-quarter of joist depth.

(2) Drill joists to a maximum diameter of one-quarter of joist depth. Locate along the span, preferably centered but no closer than 2 inches to an edge.

(3) Notch studs no larger than 2½ inches square. Nail steel strap reinforcement over each notch after installing the pipe. Notches 1¼ inches square need not be reinforced.

(4) Larger cutouts in framing members require an additional 2x4 or heavier bracing be nailed on both sides of the affected member.

WHERE TO RUN PIPES -

AVOID CUTTING JOISTS JUST TO RUN PIPES - THIS WEAKENS FLOOR!

HANGER

INSTEAD TRY RUNNING UNDER CEILING, THEN HIDE WITH NEW DROPPED CEILING

IF PIPES ARE THIN ENOUGH, THEY CAN BE RUN IN BETWEEN FURRING

DON'T CHOP OUT EXCESSIVE FRAMING LUMBER

WEAK

UNLESS YOU CAN BRACE AROUND THE NOTCHES

HERE 1/8" STEEL WILL STRENGTHEN

CEILING TILES ON 1"X 3" CAN ALSO PASS PIPES

WHEN PIPES MUST RUN ACROSS JOISTS, BETWEEN FLOORS -

RUN THEM NEAR THE TOP

A DEEP NOTCH LIKE THIS THRU A JOIST IN FLOOR - -

THIS PIPE RUN IDEA LOOKS FINE, BUT IT'S NOT POSSIBLE -

- - EXCEPT ON SHORT SECTION!

THIS IS ALSO BAD FOR A STUD WALL -

- - REQUIRES AT LEAST A 2" X 4" BATTEN TO REINFORCED THE NOTCH

- - NEEDS AT LEAST 1"X 2" OR HEAVIER REINFORCING

Fixing Faucets

Leaky faucets are responsible for more wasted water than anything else. Your home center or hardware store has parts for nearly all makes.

A FAUCET THAT LEAKS a 1/16-inch stream of water wastes 100 gallons a day. Hot or cold, that is a lot of water.

Faucets are made so many different ways that fixing a leaky one is no rigid procedure. First you must get the faucet apart, then effect the repair. Most faucets, especially old ones are washer-type ones. Most of the better newer faucets are washerless and are superior in many ways.

Identification comes first. To do this take the handle off. Handle screws may be exposed, but more likely they are hidden underneath caps. Screw or pry the cap off and you can remove the screw, then the handle by pulling or prying up. Sometimes you must remove a decorative cover to expose the faucet's works. If the faucet has a packing nut, you are likely looking at a washer-type faucet.

With the water turned off, unscrew the packing nut. Then slip the faucet handle back on and twist out the spindle by turning the faucet toward "on" position. Some spindles come out along with a threaded sleeve as soon as the packing nut sleeve is unscrewed.

At the lower end of the spindle is the washer. If it is flat, or deeply grooved and hard, replace it. As a temporary cure, an old washer can sometimes be installed backwards.

Modern faucet spindles use rubber O-rings to keep water from leaking out around the stem. Older ones used packing. A stem-leaker can be cured by replacing the O-ring (available in many sizes) or installing new packing. If the spindle is partially eaten away by corrosion, it can be replaced with a new one.

If the faucet still leaks, its seat may need attention. Some seats can be screwed out and replaced. Others are refaced in the faucet.

Washerless faucets are less prone to leak and easier to fix than washer-type ones. A rubber diaphragm or a pair of metal discs hold back water flow. The washerless spindle unit is held in by a nut. Remove it and the whole works just lifts out. Sometimes a knurled cap holds the spindle in place. No wrench needed. Your dealer can probably sell you a replacement

Repairing a modern single-lever Delta faucet is easy, should one ever drip. First turn off the hot and cold water supplies to the faucet. 1. Remove the handle and unscrew the cap nut. Pull out the works. 2. Insert a small screwdriver into each of the rubber valves inside the faucet body, pull out and discard them. 3. Slip new springs and valves into their openings in the faucet, springs down. Push them all the way down into their recesses. 4. Now the reconditioned valve assembly can be installed into the faucet and pushed down the way it was before it came out. The rest of the job is simply reinstalling the chrome cap nut and running it down finger-tight. If you get any leakage around the top of the faucet, loosen the cap nut again and tighten its flange slightly before snugging it down. 5. Parts needed come in kit form.

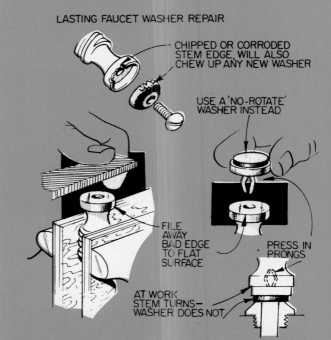

LASTING FAUCET WASHER REPAIR

CHIPPED OR CORRODED STEM EDGE, WILL ALSO CHEW UP ANY NEW WASHER

USE A 'NO-ROTATE' WASHER INSTEAD

FILE AWAY BAD EDGE TO FLAT SURFACE

PRESS IN PRONGS

AT WORK STEM TURNS— WASHER DOES NOT

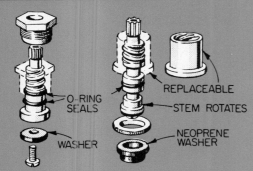

DELTA

AMERICAN STANDARD 'AQUAMIX' KITCHEN MIXER FAUCET

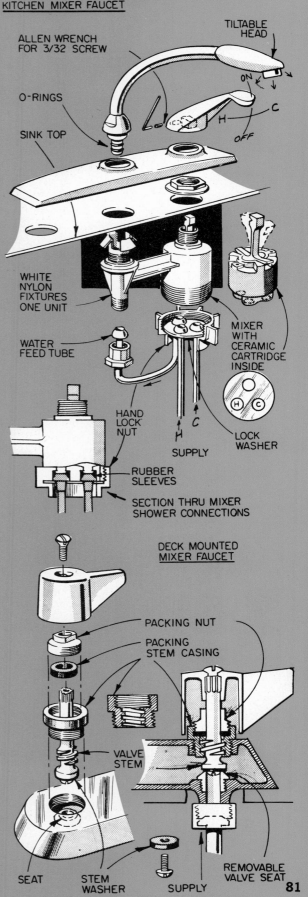

ALLEN WRENCH FOR 3/32 SCREW

TILTABLE HEAD

O-RINGS

SINK TOP

ON

OFF

H

C

WHITE NYLON FIXTURES ONE UNIT

WATER FEED TUBE

MIXER WITH CERAMIC CARTRIDGE INSIDE

H   C

HAND LOCK NUT

LOCK WASHER

H   C

SUPPLY

RUBBER SLEEVES

SECTION THRU MIXER SHOWER CONNECTIONS

DECK MOUNTED MIXER FAUCET

PACKING NUT

PACKING

STEM CASING

VALVE STEM

SEAT

STEM WASHER

SUPPLY

REMOVABLE VALVE SEAT

FAUCET STEMS ARE VARIED

O-RING SEALS

WASHER

REPLACEABLE

STEM ROTATES

NEOPRENE WASHER

TYPICAL REPLACEABLE STEMS

LONG SPINDLE TYPE

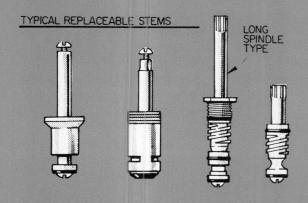

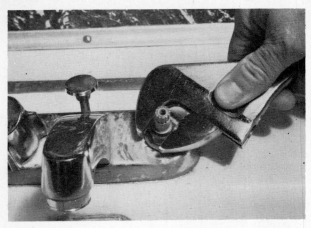 

Ordinary faucet repair starts with taking off the packing nut to see what's inside the faucet (upper left). Remove nut and spindle (upper right) exposing the washer (lower left). The damaged spindle calls for repair or replacement of both spindle and washer. Lower right, faucets with removable seats can have replacement seats installed for a complete rebuilding. Use an Allen wrench or screwdriver to remove seat.

spindle unit or else get the parts necessary to rebuild the old one.

Several types of single-lever faucets are available and if you can get the manufacturer's leaflet on service for that faucet, you are ahead of the game. Describe the faucet to your plumbing supplies dealer and see if he has an instruction sheet.

One of the most popular is the Delta, long-lived and virtually trouble-free. The older kitchen-type Delta faucets with levers coming out the rear may experience slowed flow. That is because the strainer screens may be partially blocked with sediment. Remove the spout nut, spout, and escutcheon to expose the faucet body. The brass plug on each side of center can be removed to get at the strainers. Cleaning and reassembly should cure the problem.

The newer single-lever Delta and Peerless units with top control, including tub and shower units, are repaired from the front with the handle off. Leakage around the control is a simple matter of tension adjustment. Other leakage calls for easy replacement of the rubber valves from a kit.

LAUNDRY OR UTILITY FAUCET

BONNET WITH PACKING
COMPRESSION WASHER
VALVE STEM
SEAT WASHER
VALVE SEAT
CONNECTING NUT TO SUPPLY

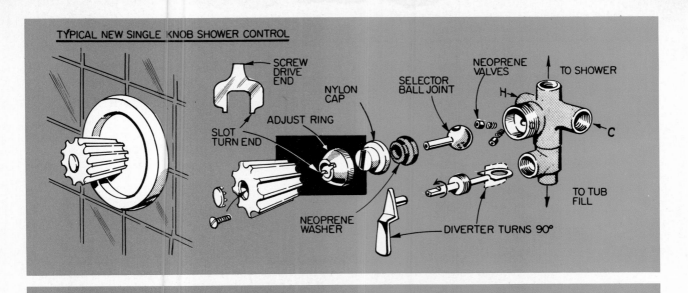

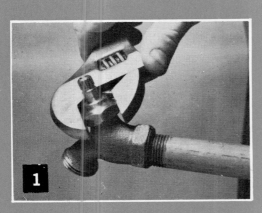

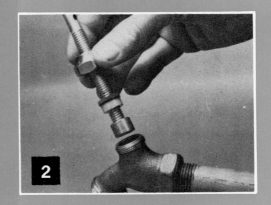

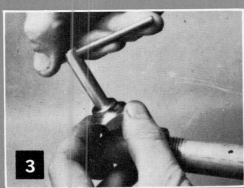

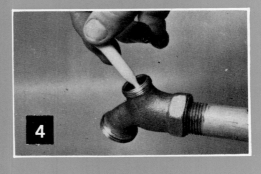

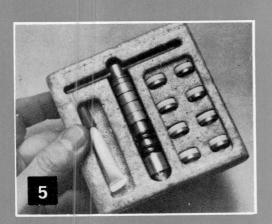

New Delrin washers and seats rejuvenate an old faucet. The Universal kit shown at the left contains everything you need. 1. Turn off the water and remove the faucet packing nut. 2. Slip the packing nut over the shaft of the seat dressing tool and install it on the faucet. Arrange the tool's washer and knurled collar so the packing nut holds it firmly against the seat. 3. Slip the tool's handle through the shaft and turn to dress down the seat. 4. Insert a new washer in the stem and dab the washer and the groove with cement. Immediately assemble the faucet and close the valve while the glue sets. No more leaks!

This may look complex, but it works the same way as most toilets with one exception. It features a Vent-Away system that removes odors before they permeate the room. Pulling the handle permits a small amount of water to flow through a jet aspirator. In ten seconds this causes a vacuum in the bowl which draws air (and odors) back through holes in the toilet rim.

Fixing Toilets

If your water closet (the fancy name for toilet) wastes water, makes unusual noises or just doesn't work, try fixing it yourself. It's really easy.

DESPITE THE EFFORT of manufacturers, the home toilet flush tank is probably the most troublesome piece of plumbing equipment in the house. One reason is that it gets so much use. The second is that it has so many automatic functions. All you do to start the flush is trip the lever once. The toilet tank then (1) continues the flush until it empties the tank (2) stops the flush when the tank water is almost gone; (3) turns on the water supply to refill the tank; (4) diverts some of the refill water to replace trap-sealing water siphoned from the toilet bowl; and (5) shuts off the water supply when tank water level reaches the correct height. The best toilet tanks also contain vacuum-breaker inlet valves that admit only air to the supply pipes should there be a back-siphonage in the water-supply system.

WATER KEEPS RUNNING

Most toilet tank troubles can be spotted by the sounds they make. The most common one, failure of the tank to shut off a minute or two after a flush, shows itself as a water-running noise. The probable cure depends on whether the tank refills or whether it stays empty after the flush. If it stays empty, the flush valve is not closing as it should. This problem is so com-

mon that toilet manufacturers have produced all kinds of flush valve designs trying to prevent it. And they have partially succeeded.

The new designs give less trouble than the old flush-ball valve. As its lever is tripped to start the flush, the rubber flush ball is lifted by wires. Then it is held up by the outflow of water until the tank is almost empty. Then the flush ball is supposed to lower and reseat itself on the valve seat. Trouble is, the lift wire may hang up on the guide arm, or the trip lever may fail to release properly and the ball stays up. Refill water keeps coming into the toilet tank, but it flows right on out again. You have to jiggle the trip lever, or reach into the tank and lower the flush ball manually.

The cure is to ashcan the whole flush ball system, removing the guide arm, and install a more reliable rubber flapper kit. You can get one for only a little more cost than for a new flush ball. Slide the flapper down on the overflow pipe until it seats on the flush valve. Rig the furnished brass chain up to the end of the trip lever arm with a little slack and your troubles should be over for a long time. Some adjustment of flapper height may be needed to get a complete flush.

If you prefer to stick with the flush ball system, check the lift wires for hang-ups, or else

OPERATION OF TYPICAL TOILET FLUSH TANK

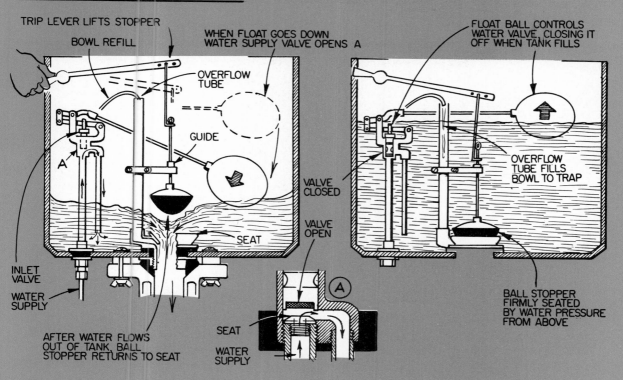

TRIP LEVER LIFTS STOPPER

BOWL REFILL

WHEN FLOAT GOES DOWN WATER SUPPLY VALVE OPENS A

FLOAT BALL CONTROLS WATER VALVE, CLOSING IT OFF WHEN TANK FILLS

OVERFLOW TUBE

GUIDE

VALVE CLOSED

VALVE OPEN

SEAT

OVERFLOW TUBE FILLS BOWL TO TRAP

INLET VALVE

WATER SUPPLY

AFTER WATER FLOWS OUT OF TANK, BALL STOPPER RETURNS TO SEAT

SEAT

WATER SUPPLY

A

BALL STOPPER FIRMLY SEATED BY WATER PRESSURE FROM ABOVE

A FEW OTHER TYPES OF FLOAT VALVES (BALL COCKS) ON THE MARKET

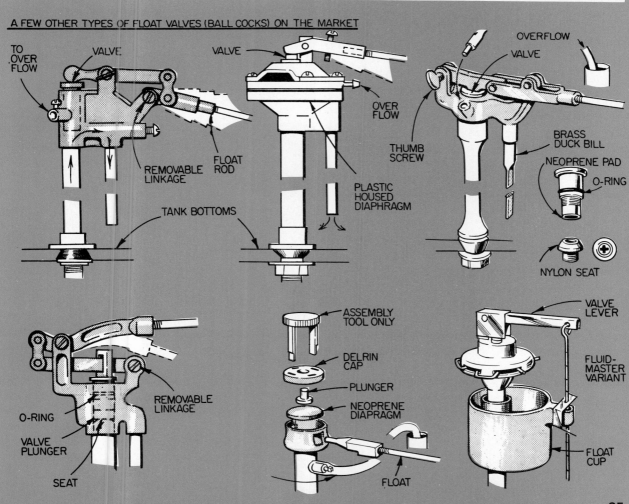

TO OVER FLOW

VALVE

VALVE

OVERFLOW

VALVE

REMOVABLE LINKAGE

FLOAT ROD

OVER FLOW

THUMB SCREW

PLASTIC HOUSED DIAPHRAGM

BRASS DUCK BILL

NEOPRENE PAD

O-RING

TANK BOTTOMS

NYLON SEAT

O-RING

VALVE PLUNGER

SEAT

REMOVABLE LINKAGE

ASSEMBLY TOOL ONLY

DELRIN CAP

PLUNGER

NEOPRENE DIAPRAGM

FLOAT

VALVE LEVER

FLUID-MASTER VARIANT

FLOAT CUP

install new ones. One thing about toilet tank repairs: lots of parts are available.

WATER RUNS, TANK FULL

If the tank fills but a water-running noise can still be heard several minutes after a flush, look closely at the float and float arm to see if they are touching any other parts of the tank. If so, bend the float arm to give clearance. If that isn't the problem, see whether the flush ball or rubber flapper is encrusted with hard-water scale. Same with the flush valve seat. Scale prevents a tight seal. You can either clean or replace; new valve seats are available in brass or plastic.

If water is running over the top of the overflow pipe, bend the float arm down to lower the water level.

A leaking ball cock valve can be the cause of water running sounds. Remove the screws from the lever mechanism, take it apart and pull out the ball cock valve with pliers. Check the valve's washer and seat. Bad washer? Install a new one, or a new ball cock valve. It pulls out with pliers. Damaged or scale-encrusted seat? Replace the whole float valve assembly in the tank hole. It's an easy task.

Look at the toilet bowl refill tube, the one coming out the top of the float valve and entering the top of the overflow pipe. It should not reach below tank water level or it will siphon water out of the tank. Bend it upward to correct.

If all else fails, you can replace everything in the tank for not too much money.

WATER LEVEL

The tank water level after refill should be ¾-inch below the top of the overflow tube. If different from this, a water level will be marked on the side of the tank. To lower the level, bend the float arm down. Bend up to raise the level. Check for float and arm binding before replacing the tank cover.

PARTIAL FLUSH

An incomplete flush is caused by the rubber flush ball or rubber flapper not getting a high enough lift to stay up. Bend the lift wires, or shorten the chain, if necessary, to get a higher lift.

SPLASHING SOUND

If, during refill, you hear splashing noises coming from the tank, see if the refill tube has slipped out of the overflow pipe; its water will then be running directly into the tank. Thus the bowl's trap-sealing water cannot be replaced

Sure cause of small toilet tank leaks is a misaligned flush ball guide arm. Loosen the arm screw-clamp and push the arm so it holds the ball lift wire vertically over the flush ball seat.

after a flush. The cure is to replace the refill tube in the overflow pipe.

TILTING-BUCKET

The newer tilting-bucket flush valves are pretty reliable. If they give problems, it's probably because of binding against the float arm, trip lever, or at the hinge. Check and bend the parts out of the way. The float arm and trip lever can be bent to get them out of the way. Cleaning should cure any hinge-binding problems.

A no-flush with any type of flush valve makes for a self-guiding repair. Usually when you remove the tank cover, you'll find a broken trip-strap, wire, or chain. You can fix them temporarily with cord.

Besides the standard ball-cock float valves you can get a flush control called the Fluidmaster. Made of plastic, it eliminates the float entirely. Water level is controlled by pressure within the unit. It also does away with gurgling sounds during tank refill. Most dealers have them as replacements that fit in your present toilet tank.

SAVING WATER

Putting a brick in the toilet tank to save on flush water is a much publicized gimmick. It is supposed to lower the water capacity of the toilet tank. The thing is, unless you place the brick vertically, it is practically useless. It rests mostly below the lowtide water level of your tank, and thus has little effect. Placed vertically, it gets in the way of the float ball. A much better method to save on water is to bend the float arm down and lower the tank water level. Try lowering it half an inch a week until you begin experiencing incomplete flushes. Then raise it back to the last successful spot and leave it. This way you'll be getting the most efficient use of flush water without any waste.

Small leaks in tank valves may be hard to detect, yet they can waste lots of water. To find them, touch a piece of paper to the back of the bowl several hours after a flush. It should be dry.

Scouring lime encrustations off the flush valve seat with steel wool may be preferable to replacing the valve. These build-ups prevent a tight seal between flush ball and seat, let water leak.

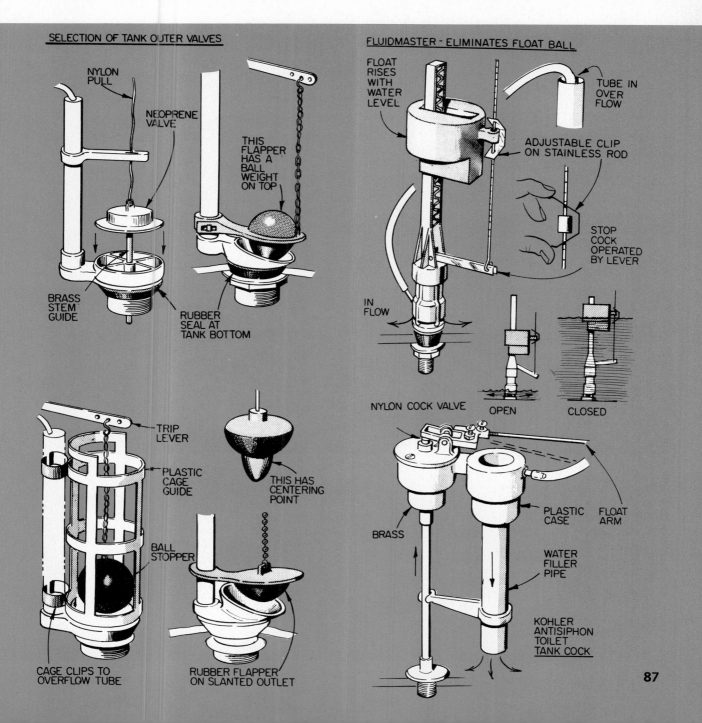

SELECTION OF TANK OUTER VALVES

NYLON PULL

NEOPRENE VALVE

THIS FLAPPER HAS A BALL WEIGHT ON TOP

BRASS STEM GUIDE

RUBBER SEAL AT TANK BOTTOM

TRIP LEVER

PLASTIC CAGE GUIDE

THIS HAS CENTERING POINT

BALL STOPPER

CAGE CLIPS TO OVERFLOW TUBE

RUBBER FLAPPER ON SLANTED OUTLET

FLUIDMASTER - ELIMINATES FLOAT BALL

FLOAT RISES WITH WATER LEVEL

TUBE IN OVER FLOW

ADJUSTABLE CLIP ON STAINLESS ROD

STOP COCK OPERATED BY LEVER

IN FLOW

NYLON COCK VALVE

OPEN

CLOSED

PLASTIC CASE

FLOAT ARM

BRASS

WATER FILLER PIPE

KOHLER ANTISIPHON TOILET TANK COCK

Stopping Leaks

No pipe or plumbing system is leakproof. Until you can make a permanent repair, here are some stop-gap measures.

Commonly available half-diameter clamp-type pipe patch comprises a metal shield that's tightened over a soft rubber gasket to seal off leaks in pipes. Get the right size to suit the leaky pipe.

THE REAL CURE for a leaking pipe, fitting, or tank is to remove and replace the faulty part. This may eventually be what you'll do. However, it might be convenient to get months or years of additional service by patching the leak. Most exposed leaks lend themselves to this treatment with a variety of commercial and homemade leak-stopping methods.

Leaks are caused by expansion of water during freezing or by corrosion. Leaking at fittings may be due to incorrect assembly. In any case, replacement can be hard, while patching is easy. It's usually worth a try.

PIPE LEAKS

A homespun patch using a piece of tire inner tube clamped tightly around a small leak in a pipe will usually work. A crack caused by freezing needs the more extensive coverage of a commercial pipe-clamp patcher or a build-up of epoxy material over the leak. Either method will last until corrosion enlarges the opening beyond what the patch covers. But this could take years.

If the leak is in a portion of the drain-waste-vent system which has no water pressure, a tight wrapping with plastic tape when the pipe is dry can stop the leak temporarily. One tape made especially for garden hose repair withstands water better than others. Otherwise, electrical tape may be used. For health reasons a permanent repair should be made without delay.

Several types of patches for leaking water tanks use soft washers that are tightened over leaks to seal them: (left to right) toggle-type uses a drilled hole; rubber and lead washer types.

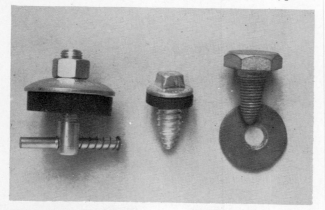

A self-tapping leak-stopper needs no drilled hole. Just screw it into the leak and let it make its own threads. The leak should stop when the rubber gasket is squeezed against the tank wall.

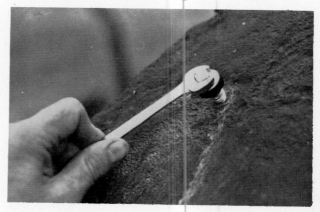

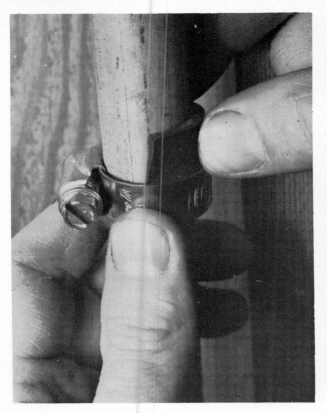

Home-made pipe patch from a piece of tire inner tube and a worm-drive screw clamp will seal off most tiny leaks. Hold the rubber over the leak, slip the clamp onto it and then tighten securely.

Heavy-duty clamp for stopping leaks in larger pipes can be bought in sizes up to the largest you'll have to work on. A stainless steel band is drawn tightly around pipe when nut is turned.

Of course, the real cure for a leaky pipe is to cut out the damaged area and install a new piece.

LEAKY FITTINGS

Two-part epoxy glue makes a good lasting patch for a leaking fitting. The area of the leak should be dry and clean. Turn the water off before you mix the epoxy. Apply it liberally working it onto the metal around the leak. Get it as thick as possible over the leak to hold against water pressure. Plastic pipe should be scuff-sanded before patching. Allow overnight curing at room temperature before turning the water on. The use of 5-minute epoxy glue will speed things considerably, but its pot-life is short.

HOLES

Water storage tanks with accessible leaks—not water heaters with their insulated jacketing–can be saved temporarily with self-tapping repair plugs. Several types are available. Screw one of them into the rusted-out opening and it seats against a gasket. One type uses a toggle system and is inserted after drilling out the hole to accept the toggle.

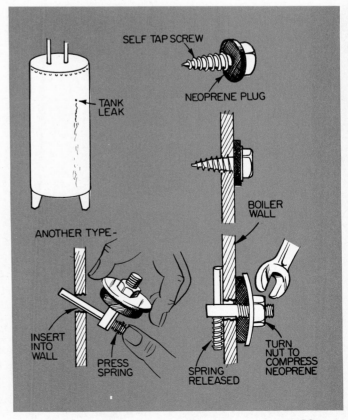

89

A complete set of plumbing maintenance tools is no big thing. Here are tools you'll find handy for unclogging drains, as well as changing fixtures and repairing faucets. (You'll also need the basic tools). At top is a curved toilet auger. Familiar plumber's force cup is below that. Also, (l. to r.) are self-storing drain auger, basin wrench, seat-dressing tool and combination fixture wrench. A must for home owners.

Tips on Unclogging

If chemical drain cleaners don't work, you must resort to mechanical methods plus some ingenuity.

THE CLOGGED DRAIN is such a common occurrence that chemical firms make millions selling drain-opening potions. Some work, some don't. It would be wonderful if there were a chemical that would solve all clogged-drain problems. However, some clogs involve more than pouring a bottle of liquid down the drain. You'll do best if you tackle a clogged drain in easy steps. Start with the least troublesome method and work toward the most effective method.

Most clogs are caused by a mixture of soap residue, hair, grease, and hard-water scale. Favorite places for blockage build-ups are inside fixture traps and at sharp turns in waste and drain pipes. A clog can even develop as far away as in the house-to-street sewer pipe. In this case, all house plumbing backs up, with upstairs waste water coming out of first-floor fixtures and spilling out onto the floor. It's a mess, but usually not beyond an owner's ability to find and fix it.

MOP UP

The first step is to mop up the overflow water before it seeps down through floors and ceiling, doing damage to the house. If more keeps coming, head for the house main shutoff valve and cut off the water to all fixtures. Now sit down and think about what happened. Did one fixture drain back up? Or are other fixtures involved?

What you're trying to do is deduce where to look for the clog. Here's a checklist:

One fixture—clog probably is in fixture's trap or waste pipe.

Lavatory and tub or shower—clog probably farther down in the bathroom branch drain leading to the soil stack.

All fixtures—clog is in building drain or house sewer.

PLUMBER'S FRIEND

Most often, only a single fixture is involved and the problem is close to the fixture. Get out a rubber force cup—also called a plumber's friend. It is the quickest, easiest, and cheapest drain-unblocker made. If you get the kind with a fold-down rim, it can be used to best advantage on both fixtures and toilets. Fold the rim down for toilets, up for fixtures.

Force cups work best with several inches of hot water in the fixture bowl to serve as a seal and help melt grease. If the drain has a stopper, take it out to get full force through the drain and onto the clog. Lavatory and bathtub drains with overflow openings require plugging of the overflows with a wet washcloth; otherwise the pressure of your plunging will escape ineffectively through the overflow. Tilt the force cup to one side to fill it with water and hold it squarely over the drain. Push the handle down and pull it up about five times in succession. Work with the rhythm of the water flowing down and back in the drain to add extra push against the clog. On the final stroke, pull up hard, lifting the plunger sharply off the drain. This may send a column of water gushing up from the drain. It also exerts great back pressure on the clog and does more to loosen it than the hardest downward push could.

If several sessions at plunging don't work, put the force cup away and get out the drain-opening chemical. Many are available but whatever you use, follow the directions on the container. Powerful chemicals are involved. They can burn eyes, skin, and some can harm fixture materials. It's best to pour the chemical directly down the drain. Some claim to work even though water is still in the bowl but application directly to the drain is more effective.

If the required time goes by and the clog remains, get out the drain auger or "snake." A long flexible cable or tape, it should be pushed in past the trap, through the waste pipe and on in until you can hear it hitting against the back of the soil stack. Rotating will help clear turns and get rid of the clog. Some snakes are slim steel tapes that are pushed into the drain and pounded against the clog. This type cannot be rotated.

An auger built just for toilets contains a sharp bend at the lower end of the handle to get the auger started up the toilet trap. One costs very little and makes a worthwhile addition to the home plumbing tool line-up. A toilet auger can save toilet bowl removal by snagging and pulling back things like teddy bears and diapers that are accidentally flushed down but do not go all the way. The auger is long enough to reach the toilet's outlet horn, but no further. Most toilet troubles are in the first bend of the trap.

Drain snake that fits an electric drill rotates as it reaches into the drain to grind out clogs. Be sure to use a well-grounded or double-insulated drill around plumbing. Buy a variable speed drill.

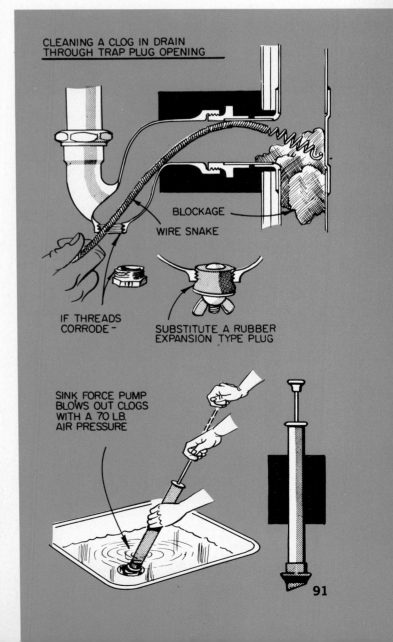

CLEANING A CLOG IN DRAIN THROUGH TRAP PLUG OPENING

BLOCKAGE

WIRE SNAKE

IF THREADS CORRODE -

SUBSTITUTE A RUBBER EXPANSION TYPE PLUG

SINK FORCE PUMP BLOWS OUT CLOGS WITH A 70 LB. AIR PRESSURE

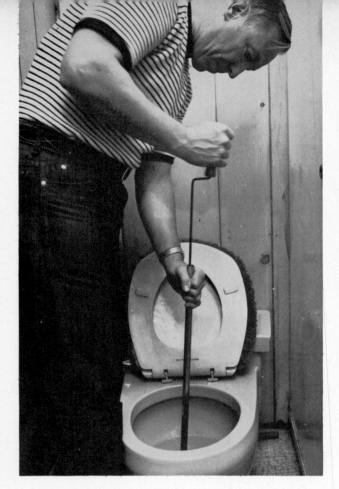

Toilet auger gets it done by reaching up the bowl's trap, grabbing clogs and pulling them out. Turning the handle rotates the snake as it is pushed out of the tool's specially bent shaft.

If you still find the drain blocked, things are getting serious. It may open up, but block again within a few weeks. This problem is often due to pipe scale. The scale gets so thick that perhaps only a very narrow passageway is left

New tool for blasting out clogs is the Woodlet's Jet Plumber. It uses an aerosol charge, which is controlled by push-handle, to open clogged drains. It works on toilets, sinks and pipes.

through the trap and waste pipes. To fix this kind of clogging, take off the trap and discard it. Be sure to put a pail under it to catch the surplus water from the bowl. Remove the waste pipe from the wall using a pipe wrench and scrape the scale out with a screwdriver before replacing it. Install a new trap. Try to rod the pipes inside the wall with your drain auger. A garden hose can be used for flushing.

When a toilet keeps clogging, and it is not a cheapie washdown type, suspect a restriction in the bowl seal at the closet flange. You will have to remove the toilet bowl to check.

BLOCKED BRANCH DRAIN

When several fixtures are involved, the clog is farther down than any single fixture's trap or waste pipe. Clogs nearly always catch in horizontal pipes where the flow is slowest or most restricted. Look in the basement or crawlspace and see what horizontal pipe serves the affected fixtures but does not serve any unaffected ones. Then trace this pipe to its upper end.

A cleanout opening should be located at the high end. Place a pail under it and take off the cleanout cover. You may have to tap it with a cold chisel to loosen it. If no water comes out, and the drains still backed up, the clog is above the cleanout. Replace the cleanout cover and move back upstairs, working in through the nearest fixture waste pipe with trap removed.

BLOCKED SEWER

If the blockage turns out to be even farther along, rod out the building drain. Your drain auger may be too short so a good substitute is a garden hose or better yet, a sewer tape. These

Water pressure operates Drain King unclogger. Attached to the end of a garden hose, the rubber body swells to the size of the drain, thus sealing it off and highly pressurizing the drain.

Through-the-roof-vent drain-cleaning is pleasant because you work neat and dry. It is most effective for reaching stoppages below where the waste pipe enters stack. 50' units are best rented.

come in 25- and 50-foot lengths and can be obtained from a tool-rental firm. They're coiled-up strips of steel, inserted in the pipe to break up clogs.

If tree roots have grown into a sewer pipe joint and blocked it, you'll have to rent an electrical auger with a root-cutting attachment. This is fed into the drain like a sewer tape. As it moves along, its cutter slices off roots inside the sewer pipe. You can also hire a professional to do this for you. Once cut, the roots can be washed along the sewer by several flushes of the toilet.

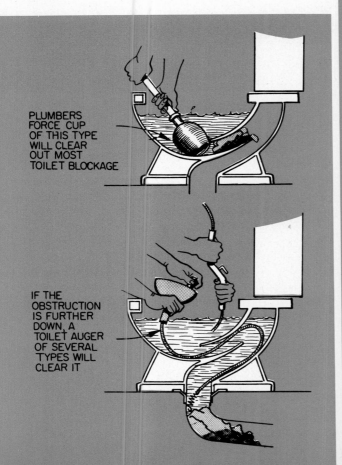

PLUMBERS FORCE CUP OF THIS TYPE WILL CLEAR OUT MOST TOILET BLOCKAGE

IF THE OBSTRUCTION IS FURTHER DOWN, A TOILET AUGER OF SEVERAL TYPES WILL CLEAR IT

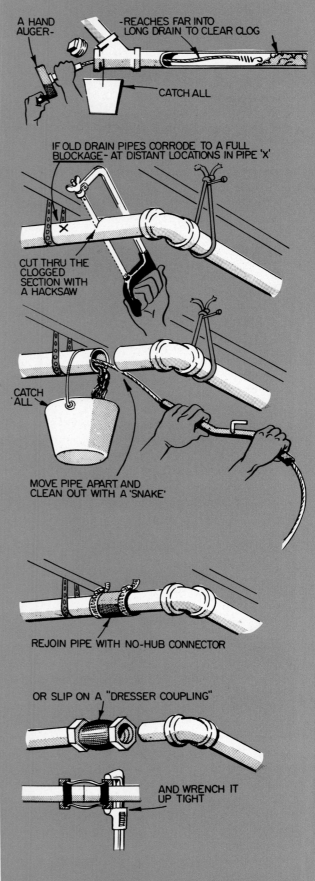

A HAND AUGER-

-REACHES FAR INTO LONG DRAIN TO CLEAR CLOG

CATCH ALL

IF OLD DRAIN PIPES CORRODE TO A FULL BLOCKAGE- AT DISTANT LOCATIONS IN PIPE 'X'

CUT THRU THE CLOGGED SECTION WITH A HACKSAW

CATCH ALL

MOVE PIPE APART AND CLEAN OUT WITH A 'SNAKE'

REJOIN PIPE WITH NO-HUB CONNECTOR

OR SLIP ON A "DRESSER COUPLING"

AND WRENCH IT UP TIGHT

93

Hot-Water

Hot-water heating is preferable to steam and more expensive to install than warm air. Its a real sign of quality.

Hot water boiler for a hydronic heating system is compact, taking up very little space in basement.

IF YOU WANT AN ARGUMENT, just ask a homeowner which is the best kind of home heating system: hot-water or warm-air. Each enjoys some advantages as well as suffering from some drawbacks. But the truth is that both can provide beautifully comfortable and efficient heat if properly designed, installed, adjusted, and maintained, no matter what fuel is used—gas, oil, coal, or electricity.

One big advantage of hot-water heat—also called hydronic heating—is that it puts a ring of warm radiant heat around the cold outer house walls.

Hot-water heating once used large radiators that intruded on room decor. Now small, unobtrusive modern radiators, convectors, or baseboard heaters are used. Room air is heated as it passes over the units. The new units take up much less floor space than the old ones.

Other than this, hot-water heating works pretty much the same as it used to. Water is heated in a boiler. A small pump pushes it through pipes to each room heating unit, then the water returns to the boiler to be heated again.

THERMOSTATIC CONTROL

A circulating pump (or two) is connected to the room thermostat, so when the house thermostat calls for heat, the circulating pump starts running. Hot water goes into action. Another thermostat located in the boiler starts the boiler heating when its water temperature falls below a certain point, then shuts it off when it gets hot enough. In the process of heating the house, the room thermostat and boiler thermostat work together. They are completely independent of each other; either one can be on while the other is off.

To prevent alternate too-hot and too-cool spells, the better thermostats contain tiny heat coils so when this heater-type thermostat calls for heat, low-voltage electricity flows through its heater coil. This warms the thermostatic spring, which then cycles off much sooner than it would have otherwise. Overheating is prevented. Since the air surrounding the room thermostat didn't get too hot, it cools more quickly and soon begins calling for heat again. Thus underheating is prevented, too. A heater-type thermostat gives brief bursts of heat at a time. This makes for an even indoor temperature with fluctuations so small you don't notice them. That's comfort!

THERMOSTAT SENSE

Too many older heating systems were set up without careful thought to good thermostat location. A common problem is that they're located too high off the floor. Easy adjustment was the idea, but comfort was sacrificed. If you think about it, most of your living is done in the lower four feet of your rooms. If that half of your house is comfortable, the whole house

seems comfortable, right? For this reason, the thermostat should be placed in the comfort half of the living quarters. The recommended height is 2 to 4 feet above the floor. Since a 2-foot level puts it down where children can fiddle with it and dogs can lick it, the best bet is to put it about 3 feet above the floor. Over a sofa or chair is a good spot. These guides apply to warm-air and other heating methods as well as to hot-water.

Never put a thermostat on an outside wall. It will read the cold coming in through the wall and be adversely affected. Also, don't put a thermostat in a draft, as near the front door or underneath a window. The cold will trigger it needlessly. On the other hand, you don't want

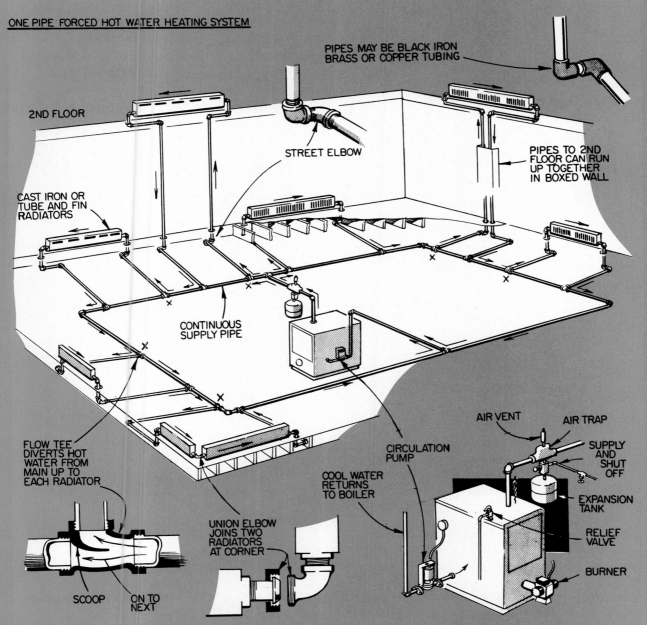

ONE PIPE FORCED HOT WATER HEATING SYSTEM

PIPES MAY BE BLACK IRON BRASS OR COPPER TUBING

2ND FLOOR

STREET ELBOW

PIPES TO 2ND FLOOR CAN RUN UP TOGETHER IN BOXED WALL

CAST IRON OR TUBE AND FIN RADIATORS

CONTINUOUS SUPPLY PIPE

FLOW TEE DIVERTS HOT WATER FROM MAIN UP TO EACH RADIATOR

UNION ELBOW JOINS TWO RADIATORS AT CORNER

COOL WATER RETURNS TO BOILER

CIRCULATION PUMP

AIR VENT

AIR TRAP

SUPPLY AND SHUT OFF

EXPANSION TANK

RELIEF VALVE

BURNER

SCOOP

ON TO NEXT

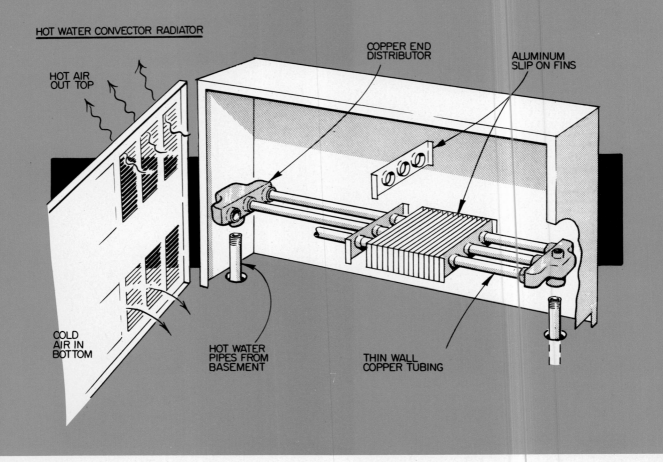

HOT WATER CONVECTOR RADIATOR

HOT AIR
OUT TOP

COPPER END
DISTRIBUTOR

ALUMINUM
SLIP ON FINS

COLD
AIR IN
BOTTOM

HOT WATER
PIPES FROM
BASEMENT

THIN WALL
COPPER TUBING

localized heat turning off the thermostat when it should be calling for more heat. So keep it away from radiant heat from a fireplace or electric light or appliance.

Poor locations are hallways, kitchens, bathrooms, laundries, bedrooms and near stairways. Good locations are living rooms and family rooms. The point is that you can easily change the location of your present thermostat if variations in heating comfort are a problem. Remove it, run the wire to the new spot and reinstall it there.

DISTRIBUTION SYSTEMS

How hot water gets around to the heating units makes a difference in heating comfort. The lowest-cost piping setup is the series loop system in which water flows through the first room heating unit, then the second, then the third and so on. It is suited to small, compact houses or mild winters. A big drawback is that with it you cannot close down one heating unit or even restrict water to it without closing down

or restricting hot water to all the other heating units. If you're installing a new system, go for one that you can control more fully.

More hydronic heating systems use the better one-pipe circulatory system. In it a single hot-water supply pipe circuits the house crawlspace, basement, or attic. When heating, it keeps up a flow of hot water. A one-way water-grabbing tee taps off to each room's heating unit, diverting some of the hot water. After flowing through the radiator, this water is piped back into the single loop. The one-pipe system suits most houses, except the largest and most rambling. If you have one of those, you'll have to opt for a better system in a new installation.

With a one-pipe system you can close down any heating unit without affecting heat to other rooms. Likewise, heating balance adjustments are possible by controlling the flow through each separate heating unit. Rooms can be warmed or cooled by effecting simple flow-control valve adjustments (see photo).

The best—but most expensive—two-pipe hot-water heating system gives the most even

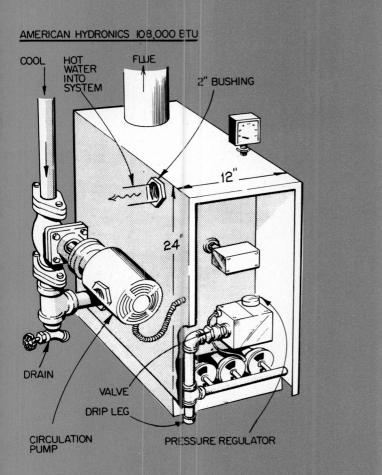

AMERICAN HYDRONICS 108,000 BTU

COOL
HOT WATER INTO SYSTEM
FLUE
2" BUSHING
12"
24"
DRAIN
VALVE
DRIP LEG
CIRCULATION PUMP
PRESSURE REGULATOR

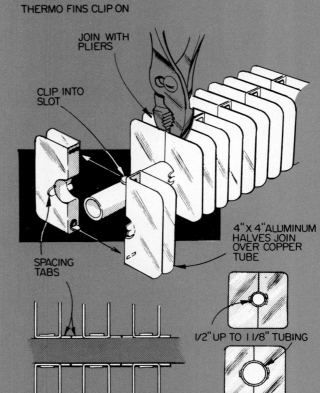

THERMO FINS CLIP ON

JOIN WITH PLIERS
CLIP INTO SLOT
SPACING TABS
4"x 4"ALUMINUM HALVES JOIN OVER COPPER TUBE
1/2" UP TO 1 1/8" TUBING

heat throughout the house. In it hot water is piped to each radiator through a supply loop. It returns to the boiler through a return loop. It takes more pipes, but each radiator gets its water undiminished in temperature. It will heat any house comfortably. Radiators in rooms that are unoccupied may be closed off. Full heating balance adjustments may be made without affecting the rest of the room units.

Hot-water also may be used in radiant heating systems with the coils embedded in the floor or ceiling of each room. These are slow to heat up, but they give the most even, comfortable heat of all. They're also the most costly system. Radiant units can even be installed in concrete basement floors. Polystyrene foam insulation should be placed underneath the slabs to prevent heat loss to the ground. Flexible copper pipes should be used for the embedded heating coils. Calculations—how many coils, what size, how long, and coil arrangement into panels—are for a heating expert to make. You can do the installation, however.

Hot-water heating lends itself to zone-control

Below, radiant copper heating pipes that will be embedded in the plaster ceiling of this house provided what's said to be the most comfortable in home heating. This is a hot-water system.

BURNHAM HOT WATER OR STEAM
CAST IRON FLOW THROUGH TYPE

FIVE
TUBES

UNION

"BASE-RAY"

PIPES FROM
BASEMENT

END

FINS

CAST IRON
HOT WATER
RADIANT HEAT

JOINS OTHER
SECTIONS

Hot-water heating boilers are now so small and inconspicuous that they can be ignored in a basement remodeling and not prove offensive to the decor. Fuel, hot-water, vent pipes are painted.

in which separate thermostats are used in certain rooms or areas of the house. When that area is warm enough—perhaps from the sun's rays—the zone thermostat cuts water circulation to it. Other rooms are unaffected. In fact, zone control of hot-water heating is so flexible and simple that you could easily add it to every problem room in the house. Such rooms are likely to be south-facing ones that are largely heated by the sun during the day but get cold at night. Got any like that? To zone-control it, simply put a thermostat in the room on an inside wall and where the sun cannot shine on it. Feed it low-voltage juice from the main thermostat, and wire a low-voltage solenoid water valve in the water line to the room's heating unit. (It won't work with a one-pipe system.) When that room needs heat, the thermostat will say so. The valve will open. When it doesn't, the valve will get no electricity and close.

Other problem rooms are kitchens and those with fireplaces that furnish part-time heat. Of course, zone control can be only partially effec-

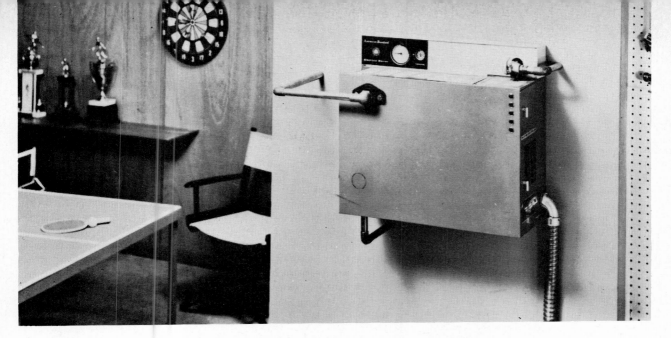

Can you believe that this tiny wall-mounted boiler (right) can heat a whole house? That's because it's electric. No fuel vent pipes or chimneys are required, just a water inlet and outlet, plus the electrical lead-in wire coming from the house's service entrance. Electrically heated homes, because of the higher cost of energy, should be tighter and well insulated with 6″ foil-faced fiber-glass batts in the ceiling, 4″ in walls.

Left, hydronic boiler is piped to an expansion tank, shown at the top of the photo, which lets water in the system expand as it is heated. About once a year, a pail of water should be drawn from bottom of expansion tank through the drain valve provided.

Balancing valves located in the pipe run to each radiator let the hot water system be adjusted so that each room heats to the desired temperature. If some rooms are cooler than you'd like, while others run too hot, find their individual balancing valves and make the adjustments with a screwdriver.

tive in rooms that are open to other rooms. A heating supplies dealer should be able to fix you up with the parts you need for zone control.

Hydronic heat extras, such as an immersion water heater, bathtub heater, and swimming pool heater, may be used, if the boiler is sized for the additional load. Naturally the more you do with your hot-water heating system, the higher your heating bill will be. Economy, rather than comfort, may be your wish.

MAINTENANCE

Unless automatic vents are used, the radia-

tors must have any accumulated air in them vented off. To do this, go around to each unit, remove the cover, if any, and open the vent valve until water begins spurting from it.

Unless your system has an automatic fill valve, the water level should be checked occasionally and the system filled to proper level. Drawing a pail of water from the expansion tank now and then will help to remove sediment. Occasionally the boiler may need draining and flushing.

If the circulating pump motor has oil openings, these should be oiled periodically. Heating units may need cleaning to retain efficiency. Remove the covers and use a vacuum cleaner brush attachment.

Warm-Air

A forced warm air system is simple and trouble-free. Here's how it works.

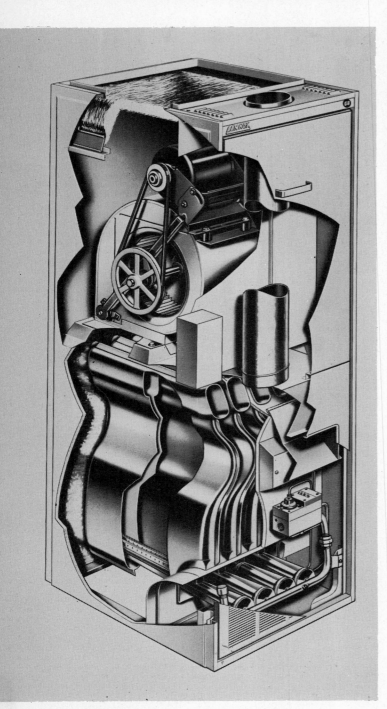

Parts of a Lennox furnace are visible in this cutaway drawing. Burners are at bottom. Heat exchangers above them lead fumes out, transfer heat to air. Blower, motor and filter are at top.

WARM-AIR HEATING, also called forced-air, uses air ducts to distribute heated (or cooled) air to each room. The old-time (pre-1930) system had no air-circulating blowers and relied on the basic principle that warm air rises to distribute heat from the furnace to the upstairs rooms. Their ducts were huge; 12 to 18 inches in diameter was no uncommon. These antiquated systems had little to recommend them except that no blower (or electricity) was needed if the fuel was coal or wood.

Modern forced-air systems are by far the most popular for home heating because of a number of reasons. First, a well engineered system in which the ducts are sized correctly to ensure each room or area will receive the recommended CFM (Cubic Feet per Minute) of air can be easily adapted for air conditioning to provide year-round comfort. Second, a forced-air system can be easily equipped with an electronic air filter and a humidifier to provide the ideal indoor climate. Third—and this is a major consideration with project and custom houses alike—warm-air systems are more economical to install than comparable hot water systems.

The heating unit for a warm-air system is called a furnace. The furnace contains a gas or oil-fired burner or electric resistance heating element, plus a squirrel-cage blower driven by an electric motor. Every furnace has a hot-air supply side and a cold-air return side. The blower and an air filter are located in the return side. Hot- and cold-air plenum chambers connect between the furnace and the house air ducts.

A humidifier is mounted in the supply duct to add moisture to the air that has been heated, while the filter (or electronic air cleaner) is located in the return.

TYPES OF DISTRIBUTION

Since warm-air heating is most popular for residences, many variations on the distribution problem have been devised. The ducts must be larger than hot-water heating distribution pipes; therefore, their installation is not as simple. The kind of warm-air system used also depends on the space available for locating the furnace. A basement furnace rests on the floor and uses basement ceiling ductwork to get its

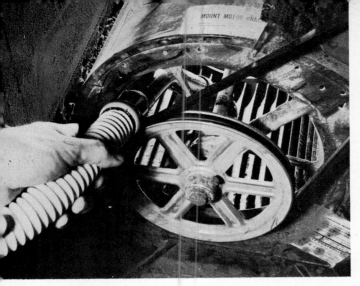

At least once a year the furnace blower should be cleaned. Do it with a vacuum cleaner hose attachment, but be sure to turn off electricity to the furnace first. Lube and set belt tension.

Better comfort results when the air is distributed around the perimeter of the home. Six-inch and larger circular ducts are very popular because they are both economical and easy to install.

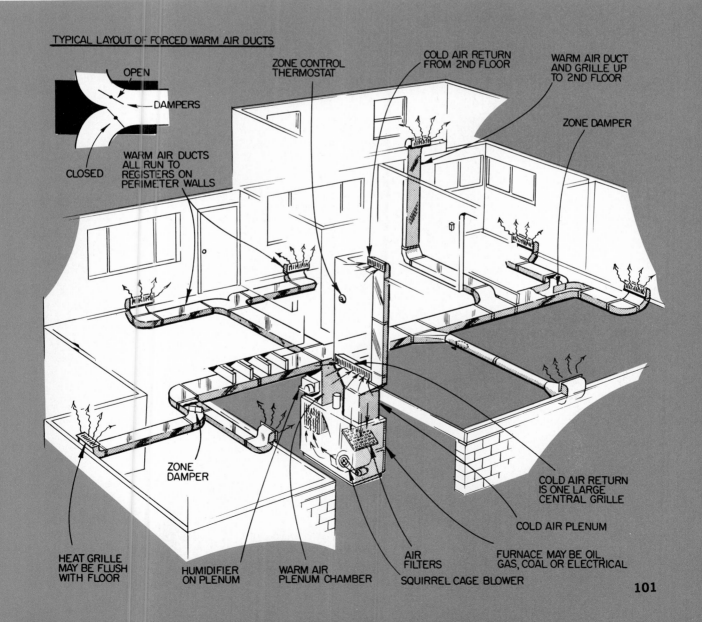

TYPICAL LAYOUT OF FORCED WARM AIR DUCTS

OPEN

DAMPERS

CLOSED

WARM AIR DUCTS ALL RUN TO REGISTERS ON PERIMETER WALLS

ZONE CONTROL THERMOSTAT

COLD AIR RETURN FROM 2ND FLOOR

WARM AIR DUCT AND GRILLE UP TO 2ND FLOOR

ZONE DAMPER

ZONE DAMPER

HEAT GRILLE MAY BE FLUSH WITH FLOOR

HUMIDIFIER ON PLENUM

WARM AIR PLENUM CHAMBER

AIR FILTERS

SQUIRREL CAGE BLOWER

COLD AIR RETURN IS ONE LARGE CENTRAL GRILLE

COLD AIR PLENUM

FURNACE MAY BE OIL, GAS, COAL OR ELECTRICAL

In mild climates and for vacation houses a floor furnace does a creditable job of heating, as long as rooms to it are open. Simply saw a framed opening for it in floor and lower into place.

warm air around and its cold air back. Then, the heat outlets—registers—are located in the first floor around the perimeter of the house. Heating ducts radiate from the furnace directly to these.

Second-story heating calls for ducts going up through house walls, which slightly complicates installation. Heating a long, rambling ranch house with warm-air involves a large central duct called an extended plenum. Room air ducts take off from the extended plenums. As

Adding more heat outlets in a room along the outside wall can increase comfort. Mark the floor with the register in place, then cut out with a jig saw. Boot and duct come from the plenum.

you might surmise, this is called an extended plenum system.

Cold air must be taken from the rooms and returned to the furnace for reheating. This is usually done by one or more large wall or floor grilles, located nearly above the furnace.

In a large, rambling house a single cold-air return may not be enough, so separate duct work must then be provided to lead the cold air back to the furnace.

OTHER SYSTEMS

Crawlspace homes can have warm-air heat using a horizontal furnace that is hung from the joists in the crawlspace. While concrete-slab-floor houses use what is called a counter-flow furnace to draw cold air in at the top and to force warm air out the bottom into a system of ducts cast right into the concrete floor. The perimeter loop system of ducts is often used in slab houses with counter-flow furnaces. Ducts radiate from the floor hot-air plenum to a continuous loop of ducts around the outside walls of the house. Floor outlets tap directly into the ducts to supply air to each room. One minor advantage to this type of system is a heated floor.

A warm-air furnace may also hang below the floor in a crawlspace or the ceiling in an attic. The furnace may be installed in a closet-like room or in a utility room. In fact, some areas can be heated without ductwork.

An excellent warm-air distribution method is the crawlspace-plenum system. It can be used to heat a one-story house built over a crawlspace sealed off from the outdoors and its floor covered with plastic sheeting, dry sand or vermiculite. A counter-flow furnace is used on the first floor above the crawlspace. It blows warm air down into the crawlspace. The warm-air plenum is fitted with short directional pipes that merely aim air toward the outer walls of the crawlspace. Floor outlets around the perimeter of the house open into the crawlspace and let heat into the rooms. A single cold-air return above the furnace brings air back into the unit. Furnace adjustments must keep crawlspace temperature below 100° and floor temperature under 80°.

Not only does the crawlspace-plenum system eliminate much ductwork, but it spreads a warming layer of heated air beneath the floor. Some heat is lost through crawlspace walls, but if well insulated this isn't enough to matter much. Not all codes approve this system.

MAINTENANCE

Most frequent maintenance to a warm-air heating system is cleaning the filter. Some can be removed, washed, and replaced. Others are simply discarded and replaced with new filters. Most stores sell filters in the popular sizes. A clogged air filter can reduce heating and comfort and efficiency by blocking good air circulation.

Likewise, heating registers need cleaning. So does the blower's squirrel cage. Shut off power to the furnace and do it with a vacuum cleaner attachment. Blower belt tension should be checked at the same time, and motor oil holes should be lubricated once a year, if they aren't permanently lubed. Don't over-oil. And if you come across a duct joint that leaks air, tape it up with duct tape.

As with all systems, the gas or oil burner should be inspected and adjusted if need be but this is a job for a professional.

CAC ADJUSTMENT

While they consume electricity, all warm-air heating systems work best when set for continuous air circulation (CAC). CAC makes the blower run slowly but continuously whenever the outdoor temperature falls below about 45°. It minimizes temperature fluctuations inside the house, lowers blower noise and provides maximum comfort from the system.

Under CAC, fan speed is set to maintain a 100° temperature rise through the furnace while the burner is operating. A limit control cuts off the burner should plenum temperature reach a dangerous high. This setting is not adjustable. Blower cut-in and cut-out points are adjustable, and these are used in adjusting for continuous running of the blower.

Zone control of warm-air systems is managed with a temperature-controlled air damper inside the ducts to certain rooms. It requires professional installation.

Warm air systems need to be balanced while in full operation on a very cold sunless day. Rooms that get too hot are dampered down to reduce heat reaching them. Rooms that get too cool are opened up to let more heat reach them. This is a job you can best do. Find the damper for each duct run. Normally, it is located near the hot-air plenum. A screw and locking nut stick out through the duct wall. If no duct dampers are provided, balance dampering may be done with adjustment screws at the registers. Make adjustments a little at a time, allowing an hour or two for the system to normalize before checking room temperatures again.

Damper position is indicated by the direction of the screwdriver slot in the damper shaft. Slot parallel to the duct opens it wide. Slot across the duct closes it fully.

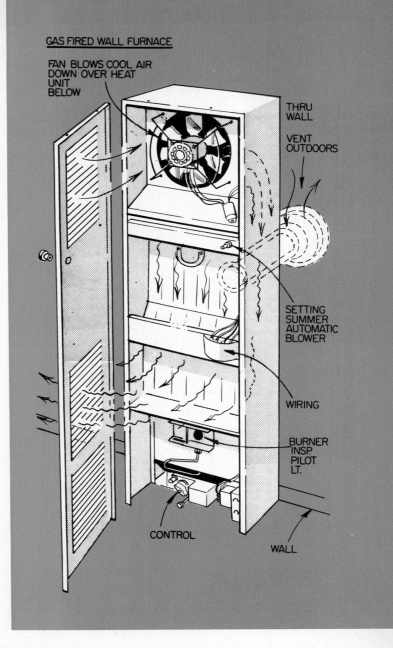

GAS FIRED WALL FURNACE

FAN BLOWS COOL AIR DOWN OVER HEAT UNIT BELOW

THRU WALL

VENT OUTDOORS

SETTING SUMMER AUTOMATIC BLOWER

WIRING

BURNER INSP PILOT LT.

CONTROL

WALL

Only with forced warm air heat can you have a built in electronic air cleaner. One of these units removes air particles as small as smoke and pollens; indispensable for hay fever sufferers.

Massive, unsightly radiators are a sure sign of an old steam or hot water system. In a steam layout, one of the biggest problems is to keep the radiator valves working right. An overnight soaking in vinegar is an old timer's remedy, followed by cleaning with a wire or broomstraw. This radiator was actually part of an old steam system but was converted to hot water.

YOUR HEATING SYSTEM: Steam

If you happen to move into a large old house with a steam system, you should be ready for all problems.

NOT MANY HOMES still use steam heat. Hot water and warm air do the job cheaper and in many ways better. But, if you have lived in a home with steam heat, you know that it is effective heat.

Steam heat works a lot like hot-water heat except that no circulating pump is needed because steam makes its own circulating pressure. Larger pipes are necessary to circulate a large volume of steam. Water is heated in a boiler until it boils. (No boiling occurs in a hot-water system's "boiler.") The steam thus created flows through 2-inch and larger pipes to steam radiators in the rooms. Each of these has an air bleeder valve that lets trapped air out of the system to make way for steam. But when steam hits the valves, they close. As steam's heat is used up by the radiator, the steam condenses into hot water and runs down through some of the same pipes it came up in and through a smaller return pipe and back to the boiler. Steam heat gets around to the rooms faster, but with fluctuations in temperature.

MAINTENANCE

Moreover, a steam system requires more attention than a hot-water system. The air vents, in time, become plugged and either fail to open or fail to close. If they won't open, steam cannot displace air in the radiator and it does not get warm. If a valve doesn't close, steam escapes and adds to house humidity sometimes desirably, sometimes not. Anyway, the hissing sound is a feature of steam heat. The valves should be unscrewed and soaked in vinegar overnight, then flushed out with water. Or they can be replaced with new valves.

Leaking radiator valves can be fixed by tightening the packing nut or adding more packing. Radiators that give off a "steam hammer" sound when heating are partially blocking with water. Put wooden blocks under the legs opposite the valve to drain water and leave them in place. Steam escaping from radiators eventually means that boiler water must be replaced or it will boil dry. A water glass on the boiler shows the level of its water so make certain it is checked regularly to maintain the correct level. If the water level glass becomes cloudy so you can't read it, close the stopcocks and remove and replace it with a new glass tube. Opening a valve lets fresh water into the boiler to refill the system. There should be a backflow-prevention device between the fill valve and the house water system, to eliminate that as a cross-connection. Few systems have one. Consult your plumber about making an installation. It's not a good do-it-yourself job.

A steam boiler also contains a pressure gauge. Steam pressure, to reach the radiators properly, runs from 2 to 10 psi. At 12 psi pressure is getting too high. At 15 psi a safety relief valve similar to the one atop your water heater should blow off to release excess pressure and keep the boiler from exploding. The operation of this relief valve should be checked periodically by pulling the lever.

Annually, the steam system needs to be drained and refilled with fresh water. Sometimes anti-leak boiler compounds and anti-rust compounds are added to boiler water to reduce water problems, such as scale, from harming the boiler.

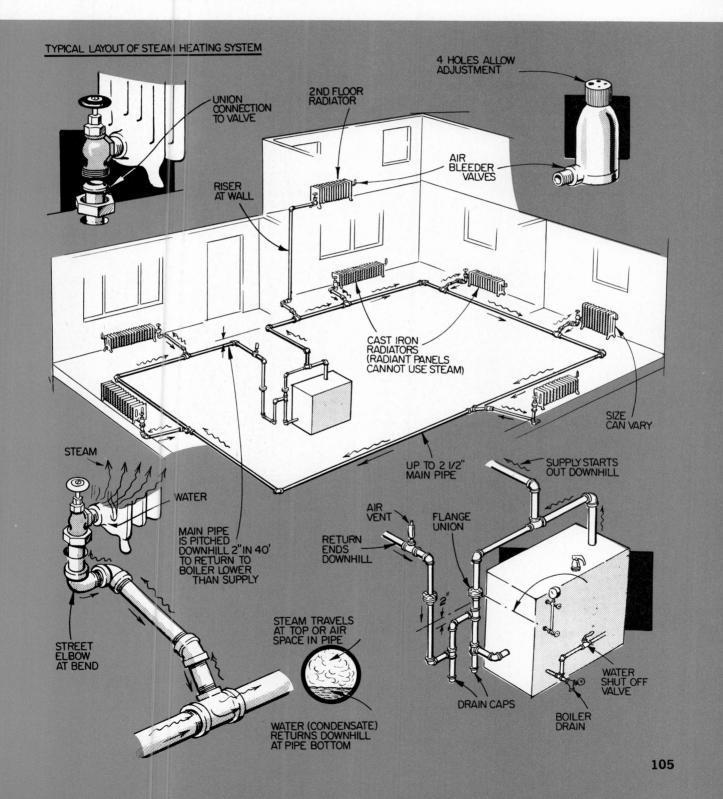

TYPICAL LAYOUT OF STEAM HEATING SYSTEM

UNION CONNECTION TO VALVE

2ND FLOOR RADIATOR

4 HOLES ALLOW ADJUSTMENT

AIR BLEEDER VALVES

RISER AT WALL

CAST IRON RADIATORS (RADIANT PANELS CANNOT USE STEAM)

SIZE CAN VARY

STEAM

WATER

MAIN PIPE IS PITCHED DOWNHILL 2" IN 40' TO RETURN TO BOILER LOWER THAN SUPPLY

UP TO 2 1/2" MAIN PIPE

SUPPLY STARTS OUT DOWNHILL

AIR VENT

FLANGE UNION

RETURN ENDS DOWNHILL

STREET ELBOW AT BEND

STEAM TRAVELS AT TOP OR AIR SPACE IN PIPE

WATER (CONDENSATE) RETURNS DOWNHILL AT PIPE BOTTOM

DRAIN CAPS

WATER SHUT OFF VALVE

BOILER DRAIN

Lowering a precast concrete septic tank into the ground is a routine job for a truck that's equipped to-handle it. The truck delivers the tank, backs in and unloads it into the prepared hole. Most tank suppliers can provide specifications on how long, wide and deep the hole must be to allow the cables to be unhooked once the tank is in. In any case, the tank should be at least 1' to 2' below grade, especially in cold climates.

Private Sewage Disposal Systems

Nothing can be more inconvenient than a private sewage disposal system that is either too small or doesn't work. Here's what you should know.

A PRIVATE SEWAGE-DISPOSAL system can easily dispose of a couple of thousand dollars of your hard-earned money. Even more. But it beats running to the well-known little brick building with its characteristic crescent-shaped window. It's better for the environment, too. A private disposal system lets you enjoy the convenience of the city while you're living far out in the country.

The oldest and most-used sewage-disposal method is the septic system. Sewage flows through a tight sewer line from the house to the septic tank. There bacterial action decomposes both solid and liquid wastes into a clear liquid effluent. A small amount of solids accumulate in the bottom of the tank while the liquid effluent leaves the tank and flows to a seepage pit or enters a distribution box where it is divided equally among two or more seepage lines. Seepage lines are made of open jointed tiles or perforated pipes that let the effluent seep out into gravel beds and percolate into the soil, evaporate, or both.

Never allow roof or ground runoff water into a septic system. Sewage only. Seepage lines cannot be used in all instances because of the terrain or lack of yard space, so a vertical pit appropriately labeled a "seepage pit" is used. This is merely a huge hole into which a specially designed precast concrete section is lowered. The area between the concrete section and the surrounding earth is then filled with gravel and sand or a combination of both. Thus, the effluent either seeps into the bottom of the pit or into the surrounding side area. Where these special pre-cast concrete pits are not practical

If you dig digging, and your soil is not hard clay, a hand-dug septic system installation is possible. Lay out the seepage trenches downhill from the tank and dig to proper depth, no deeper than 36".

Pound grade stakes into the bottom of the trench to the exact elevation the top of the gravel fill should reach. Use a 10' 2 x 4 straightedge with a level taped to it to get the correct slope.

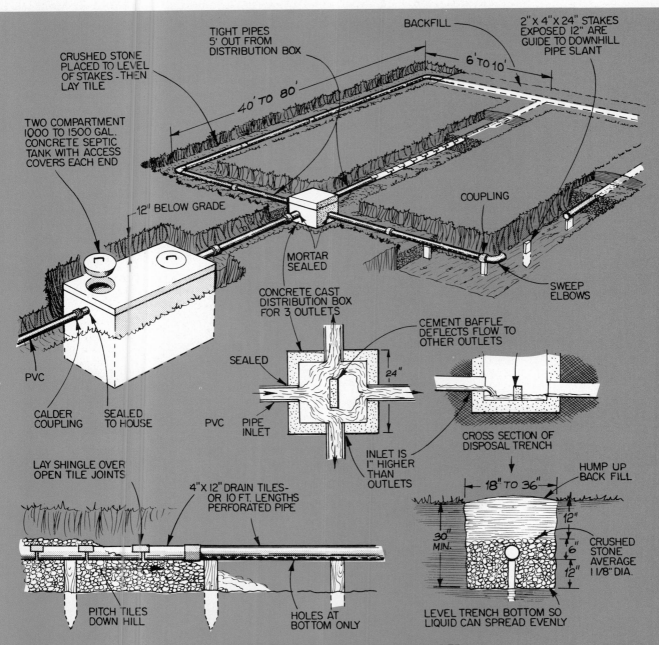

CRUSHED STONE PLACED TO LEVEL OF STAKES - THEN LAY TILE

TIGHT PIPES 5' OUT FROM DISTRIBUTION BOX

BACKFILL

2" X 4" X 24" STAKES EXPOSED 12" ARE GUIDE TO DOWNHILL PIPE SLANT

6' TO 10'

40' TO 80'

TWO COMPARTMENT 1000 TO 1500 GAL. CONCRETE SEPTIC TANK WITH ACCESS COVERS EACH END

COUPLING

12" BELOW GRADE

MORTAR SEALED

SWEEP ELBOWS

PVC

CALDER COUPLING

SEALED TO HOUSE

CONCRETE CAST DISTRIBUTION BOX FOR 3 OUTLETS

SEALED

PVC

PIPE INLET

CEMENT BAFFLE DEFLECTS FLOW TO OTHER OUTLETS

24"

INLET IS 1" HIGHER THAN OUTLETS

CROSS SECTION OF DISPOSAL TRENCH

LAY SHINGLE OVER OPEN TILE JOINTS

4" X 12" DRAIN TILES- OR 10 FT. LENGTHS PERFORATED PIPE

PITCH TILES DOWN HILL

HOLES AT BOTTOM ONLY

18" TO 36"

HUMP UP BACK FILL

30" MIN.

12"

6"

12"

CRUSHED STONE AVERAGE 1 1/8" DIA.

LEVEL TRENCH BOTTOM SO LIQUID CAN SPREAD EVENLY

TYPICAL SEPTIC SYSTEM LAYOUT FOR LEVEL SITE
(CHECK WITH LOCAL CODE)

107

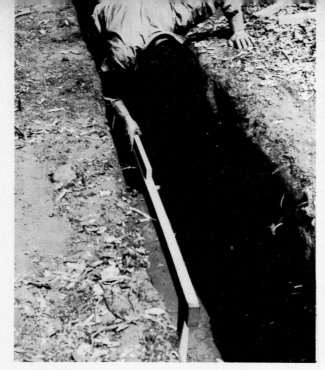

Rest the straightedge across a pair of grade stakes and adjust the height of the just-driven one until the slope meets specs. Some health officials call for dead level; others want a fall.

Haul gravel to the trenches in a wheelbarrow and dump it. Most homeowners prefer to have a contractor do the digging and materials hauling for them. A backhoe is used to dig the trenches.

for either installation or economic reasons, a perfectly adequate pit can be built with concrete blocks stacked sideways as shown in the drawings.

Because a septic tank only partially treats wastes, septic effluent is unsuitable for discharge above the ground. Much more complete treatment like that given in municipal sewage-treatment plants, is provided by the newer single-family sewage treatment plants. These aerate sewage and sometimes filter and chlorinate it to render it harmless to lakes and streams. However, they cost much more than a septic system.

The kinds of private sewage-disposal systems you can use are governed by the policies of

your local department of public health. Local health department advice should be sought; everything you install should meet its approval. A health officer may come out and help you plan a system that will work in your soil. Don't work around him or your system can be condemned. At the least, he can make you open it up for inspection, a lot of unnecessary work. The health officer can also give you the names of reliable septic disposal-system contractors, in case you prefer to leave that work to someone else.

PERCOLATION TEST

Soil porosity determines how easy it will be to get rid of effluent from your disposal system. The more porous your soil the less seepage area

Two of the most practical underground drainage and sewer pipes (below) are plastic and pitch-fiber. Plastic pipes are joined by solvent-welding just as with DWV pipes. Coat the pipe (left), then the fitting with solvent cement and push together (center), Joints in perforated seepage runs need not be welded. At right, pitch-fiber couplings are tapered to match the tapered ends of pipes. Hammer to join them together.

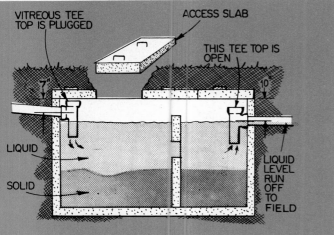

VITREOUS TEE TOP IS PLUGGED
ACCESS SLAB
THIS TEE TOP IS OPEN
7'
10'
LIQUID
SOLID
LIQUID LEVEL RUN OFF TO FIELD

is needed. Unless he is already familiar with how your soil acts under water, the health officer may require a percolation test. While some departments like to have costly engineered "perk" tests, fight for a do-it-yourself one. To do it, post-hole half a dozen four-inch diameter or larger holes spaced evenly throughout the area where your seepage field is to go. Make them about 36 inches deep. If the bottoms fill with water, abandon the site. The water table is too high for successful seepage.

Roughen or scratch the sides of the holes to present a natural surface. Remove all loose materials. Then throw about 2 inches of coarse sand or fine gravel into the bottom of each to prevent scouring. Fill each hole with water at least 12 inches over the gravel. Keep the water at this level during a 4-hour minimum (better 12-hour) saturation period. (If you have trouble getting the holes to fill at all, cheer. Your soil is very porous and you may make the percolation test right away.)

At the end of the saturation period, adjust the water to a depth of six inches. Now measure the fall in water level at 30-minute intervals for

Spread the dumped gravel evenly to the tops of the preset grade stakes, then lay 4" seepage pipe on top of the gravel. Check the slope of each length of 10' seepage pipe with a level to be sure.

Carefully join each length of seepage pipe, making certain it is in the center of the trench. Drain tiles can also be used, but they are usually more expensive than fiber pipe. Harder work, too.

PERCOLATION TEST	
PERCOLATION RATE— MINUTES IT TAKES FOR WATER LEVEL TO DROP 1 IN. IN FINAL TEST PERIOD	MINIMUM SQ. FT. OF SEEPAGE TRENCH BOTTOM AREA PER BEDROOM
2 OR LESS	85 SQ. FT.
3	100
4	115
5	125
10	165
15	190
30	250
45	300
60	350
MORE THAN 60	UNSUITABLE

SOURCE: FHA MINIMUM PROPERTY STANDARDS

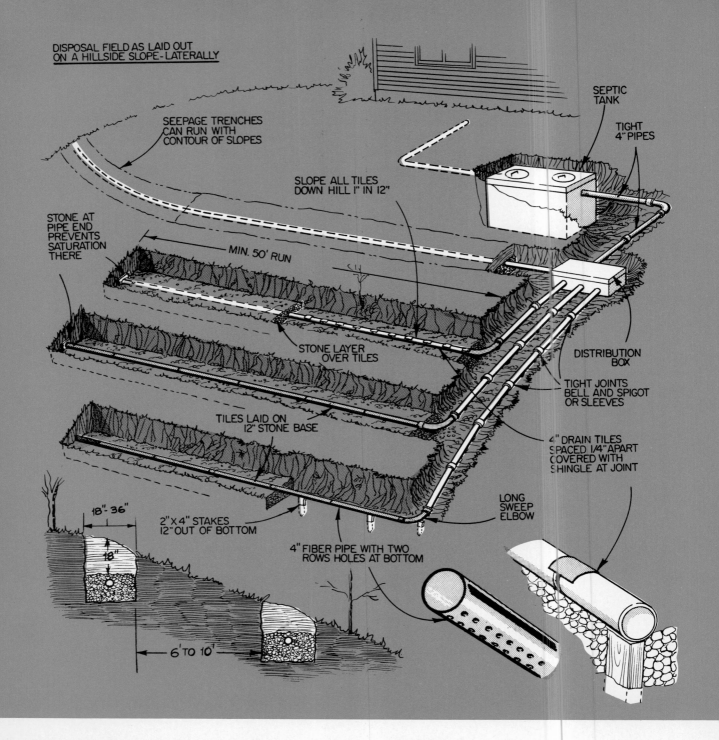

DISPOSAL FIELD AS LAID OUT
ON A HILLSIDE SLOPE-LATERALLY

SEPTIC TANK

TIGHT 4" PIPES

SEEPAGE TRENCHES CAN RUN WITH CONTOUR OF SLOPES

SLOPE ALL TILES DOWN HILL 1" IN 12"

STONE AT PIPE END PREVENTS SATURATION THERE

MIN. 50' RUN

STONE LAYER OVER TILES

DISTRIBUTION BOX

TIGHT JOINTS BELL AND SPIGOT OR SLEEVES

TILES LAID ON 12" STONE BASE

4" DRAIN TILES SPACED 1/4" APART COVERED WITH SHINGLE AT JOINT

18"- 36"

2" X 4" STAKES 12" OUT OF BOTTOM

18"

4" FIBER PIPE WITH TWO ROWS HOLES AT BOTTOM

LONG SWEEP ELBOW

6' TO 10'

four hours. If any hole is likely to run dry during the following half-hour period, refill it to six inches deep.

The time it takes for the water level to drop one inch during the final 30-minute period is called the percolation rate.

If the whole six inches of water seeps away in less than half an hour—it can happen in sandy soils—switch to 10-minute test periods and run your test over one hour instead of four. Then the time to drop one inch is the final 10-minute period is the percolation rate.

LAYOUT

Arrangement of the septic tank, distribution box, and seepage lines depends on the size, shape, and slope of your lot. Location of water wells, property lines and streams also must be taken into account. Your local health or building department will advise you on what layout is best.

A 6000-sq. ft. lot is usable for a septic system only under ideal conditions. A better minimum size is 10,000 sq. ft. (about ¼ acre). The more area the better. Follow the minimum distances

After seepage pipe or tile is in place, pack the sides and cover the top with stone. Then lay a strip of roofing paper in the trench to prevent the backfilled dirt from clogging the system.

With the roofing paper in place, you can backfill each trench by hand or with a front end loader. You can expect some settling so build a mound of dirt about 6″ over each trench. Plant grass.

shown in the drawing. The septic tank and field should be located on a down slope from the house for natural flow by gravity.

Septic tank size should be sufficient to handle all wastes carried into it. The minimum liquid capacity should be 750 gallons for two bedrooms and less; 900 gallons for three bedrooms; and 1000 gallons for four bedrooms. Houses with food waste disposals need larger septic tanks.

BUILDING THE SYSTEM

Unless you love digging, hire a contractor with a backhoe to dig the septic tank, sewer lines and seepage trenches. Have your plan laid out with stakes. Tell him the depths and slopes you need to meet health department approval and trust him to get them. The sewer should slope ¼-inch per foot. If it slopes more, make the last ten feet next to the septic tank slope no steeper than that. Specifications for slope of seepage trenches very from dead level to 6 inches per hundred feet. A slope of 2 to 4 inches in a hundred feet is reasonable. Trench width specs vary from 12 to 36 inches. A common one is 18 inches.

The hole for the septic tank should be deep

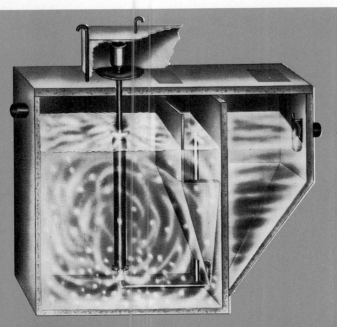

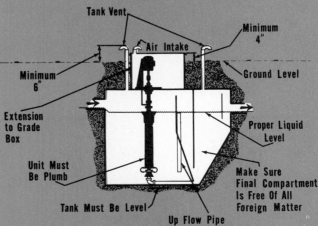

The finest sewage-disposal system available for homes is the single-family sewage-treatment plant. This one, called the "Cavitette" by Clow, aerobically treats the sewage before releasing it.

Tank Vent

Air Intake

Minimum 4″

Minimum 6″

Ground Level

Extension to Grade Box

Proper Liquid Level

Unit Must Be Plumb

Make Sure Final Compartment Is Free Of All Foreign Matter

Tank Must Be Level

Up Flow Pipe

111

Here's the lower section of a precast concrete seepage pit that usually takes the place of the built-up type shown in the drawing below. They are lifted in place with a crane at the same time the septic tank is positioned. Depending upon the porosity of the soil, sometimes two or more sections are stacked. A special cone shaped top with an access hole caps off the pit. Note how the holes slope down.

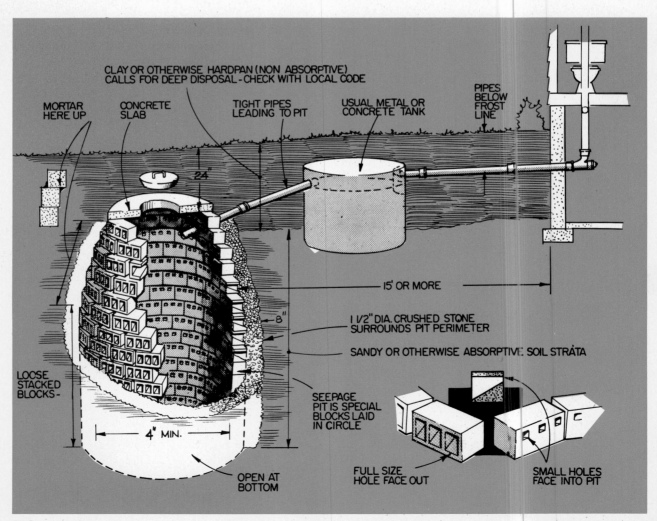

CLAY OR OTHERWISE HARDPAN (NON ABSORPTIVE) CALLS FOR DEEP DISPOSAL - CHECK WITH LOCAL CODE

MORTAR HERE UP

CONCRETE SLAB

TIGHT PIPES LEADING TO PIT

USUAL METAL OR CONCRETE TANK

PIPES BELOW FROST LINE

24"

15' OR MORE

8"

1 1/2" DIA. CRUSHED STONE SURROUNDS PIT PERIMETER

SANDY OR OTHERWISE ABSORPTIVE SOIL STRATA

LOOSE STACKED BLOCKS

4" MIN.

OPEN AT BOTTOM

SEEPAGE PIT IS SPECIAL BLOCKS LAID IN CIRCLE

FULL SIZE HOLE FACE OUT

SMALL HOLES FACE INTO PIT

enough to allow the top of the tank to be at least a foot below finished grade. In cold climates you may need two or three feet of dirt covering the top to keep from freezing.

The septic tank may be home-built of redwood, concrete, concrete block, clay tile, or bricks. Better, though, is to buy a ready-made precast concrete tank of the required size. Two-compartment units give much better action, and should be used if possible.

The seller will deliver the tank and lower it into your prepared hole in the ground. Ask him for specs on hole size.

Tank in place, run a tight sewer line from house to tank. Make connections at the tank with a coupling set up for the pipe size and type at sewer and septic tank. Normally an inverted four-inch sewer tee serves as an inlet. All pipes should be supported on unexcavated earth or on well-tamped dampened fill. Don't have soft pipes—plastic and pitch-fiber—in contact with large stones. Dig out for couplings so pipes are supported full length by the trench. Provide a cleanout opening at the house end and don't backfill until after inspection.

SEEPAGE FIELD

Run another tight line from the septic tank outlet tee to the distribution box. This is also obtainable from your local concrete products supplier. Get the distribution box outlet pipes level with each other. Test with water. Begin seepage trenches at least 5 feet from the distribution box. Set grade stakes in the seepage trenches using a 2 x 4 and level about six feet apart. Their tops should be about 12 inches above the trench bottom and sloped as you plan for the seepage pipes. Fill to the tops of the stakes even with ½- to 2½-inch gravel. When ordering gravel, allow 10 per cent for waste. One cubic yard equals about 1½ tons.

Lay four-inch seepage tiles or perforated pipes in the trenches on top of the gravel. Cover the ¼-inch joints between tiles with strips of 15-pound asphalt-saturated felt to prevent infiltration of backfill materials. Perforated pipes are laid with their twin rows of holes down. Join them with couplings. Seepage lines must not be watertight except at turns where they should be made with standard watertight drainage fittings.

Get an inspection, then fill four inches above the lines with more gravel. Lay down a layer of untreated building paper over the gravel and backfill over that with at least 12 inches of soil. Don't tamp the soil, but mound it up slightly above grade, letting it settle. After settlement, you can landscape the entire area with just

about anything but willow trees. Their roots tend to infiltrate and clog seepage lines.

Septic tank system maintenance consists of checking the sludge level in the tank every year or two. To do it, remove the tank cover and poke a 2x4 down to check. A two-compartment tank can often go 10 to 12 years without its sludge level getting more than half-way up to the scum level, the point when the tank should be pumped out.

Precast distribution boxes such as the one shown, are used when two or more seepage field lines or pits are necessary. Set the unit in place, level the holes and tamp the bottom. Then toss some dry cement in the bottom, mix slightly with the existing sand, and dampen to form a smooth surface.

Developing Your Own Water

The water that contains no fluorides, no chlorine, no pollution is the water that you develop yourself, on your own land. No other water tastes as good!

The most satisfactory source of plentiful water is usually a deep drilled well. The equipment needed for drilling usually puts it out of the home owner's reach. Well cost author $10 a foot.

IF YOU BUILD A HOUSE away from a municipal water supply, you will have to develop your own water supply. In fact, your health department may even require a source of potable house water before granting you a building permit. That source may be a shallow well, a deep well, a spring or a source of surface water such as a lake or stream. Surface water sources will require treatment, usually chlorination, before they can be considered pure enough to drink.

Look for the easiest-to-develop sources of

water first. Later, after you're settled, you can develop better ones. If there are any year-round springs on the property, this is your first consideration. Watch the use of surface water. It can become contaminated by animals, dead and otherwise, even though no people are in the area.

A continuously wet spot in the ground or on the side of a hill may be developed to provide ample water for vacation living. Actually, with adequate storage, not much water flow is needed. A half-gallon-a-minute rate of flow is fantastic! It doesn't sound like much, but it does add up to 720 gallons a day, more water than you'll need for a household.

DEVELOPING A SPRING

Enclosed is the word for tapping water from a flowing spring. You've got to get the water, contain it, and control it without exposing it to surface pollution. It can flow over rocks or sand but not over soil containing living organisms, such as black dirt. These will make the water fail purity tests. Dig away all such soil from the spring to get down to the source, which is often a crack or fault in underlying rocks.

A hillside spring's water can be tapped by digging a trench across the hill just below the spring. Lay a perforated pipe in gravel in the trench and backfill it to keep surface water out. Slope the connection pipe and connect a plastic pipe to its lower end. This should lead into a closed collection tank of at least 500 gallons. The collection tank may be made of steel or concrete. It stores an average day's supply of water for the family and provides an overflow for excess water.

If you can get at the spring's source, clean it and build a concrete or masonry box to collect the water. The box needn't be large. Fit it with a bug-tight plywood cover to prevent contamination. If the spring area is not accessible to materials, but stones are plentiful, build the spring box out of stone and a mortar mix.

A tunnel can be dug back into a hillside to collect spring water in porous material. If a spring's water comes out containing much silt, build a series of in-the-box dams to catch it before the water enters your collection pipe. Clean out behind the dams at intervals to keep the spring from silting up.

A plastic pipe can lead from the collection box (or boxes if there are several springs) to the storage tank. If your springs are high enough above the house—100 feet of elevation gives about 45 psi water pressure—you can flow the water down from the storage tank to the house.

Lowering a submersible pump and down-pipe into a drilled well can be a do-it-yourself job, but you need a heavy tripod, a hoist, and a reliable clamp. The pros do it with power equipment.

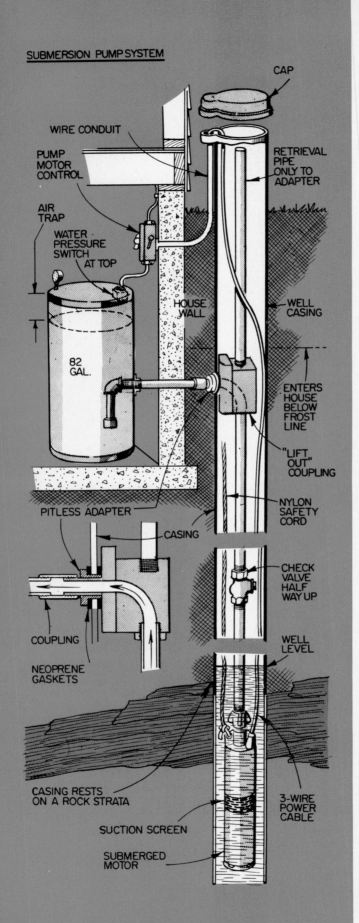

Sections of well down-pipe are joined with doped couplings. The most important tool to the job is the pipe clamp that keeps the pipes from falling in well while you make connections.

Then no pump is necessary. If the spring is not much above the house or is below it, a pump will be needed to provide enough water pressure to the house.

WELL WATER

A better source of water is a well. The simplest is a driven well, in which pointed pipe is sledge-hammered into soft loose ground. The lower end of the pipe is perforated and screened so that when it reaches the water, it can fill with water. Then you can lower a suction pipe and pump the water out. Driven wells, while they are not costly, neither reach very deep nor penetrate rocky ground. If the well point hits a rock, drilling stops. They are at their best when driven vertically or horizontally into porous ground containing water. It may take more than one driven well to collect enough water. An advantage of a horizontal well is that water flows out without pumping. Driven wells are classed as shallow wells, tap-

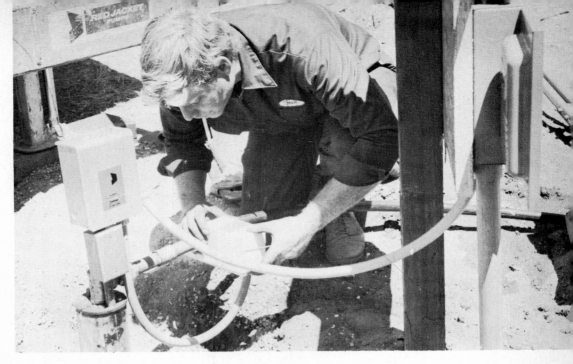

All sorts of controls are to be had for well pumps. The one being installed is a flow-shut-off switch. It stops the pump should it run out of water. A built-in timer restarts it again 15 minutes later. The control prevents possible pump motor burnout.

ping shallow ground water. Since they can easily be contaminated, shallow wells leave much to be desired.

A drilled deep well is the best. However, it's no do-it-yourself job. Hire a reputable drilling contractor. How deep you'll have to go to find underground water depends on how far down the water-bearing strata is and how much water you need. One gallon a minute is enough for the household, but 5 gallons a minute will handle most households without providing any storage. More than that can provide enough water for irrigation. Drilled wells may go straight down (most do) or laterally into a hillside. If successful, laterally drilled wells flow water out in artesian fashion. Most vertical wells must be pumped. Drillers install 4- to 6-inch well casing pipes down to solid rock.

WHERE'S THE WATER?

You can choose from among three methods to determine where to drill: proximity to the house, geology and witching. To locate the well using the geological method, you'll need a science background or a friend with one. Water-witching takes a talent that not everyone

What a joy! To have pressurized, flowing water, away from city mains where there was none before you developed it. More than 500 gallons a day is enough for successful irrigation. Water is as basic as fire.

Installing the sanitary well seal caps off the well and prevents surface infiltration from contaminating it. The seal's halves expand against the well casing when bolts are drawn down. The single pipe to a submersible pump extends through the sanitary seal.

PUMPS

has, plus a certain amount of faith on your part. I didn't believe it until I saw it work. You most likely won't either.

Water is moved out of a well or storage tank and pressurized with an electric pump. A shallow well pump will handle huge quantities of water from depths up to 25 feet. Deeper than that you need a deep well rig, either jet or submersible.

For wells, nothing beats the submersible pump. The pump and electric wires serving it are lowered onto the well casing. Control is from up top. The pump discharges into a sealed 42- or 80-gallon air tank, compressing air in the top of the tank until the desired pressure of 40 to 50 psi is reached. Then a pressure switch shuts off the pump. To prevent water from running down through the pump and back into the well, a check valve is located in the bottom of the pump. Submersible pumps are not for sandy wells.

Lower in cost are jet pumps. The motor and turbine pump are above the well with a suction pipe extending down into the water. If the water depth is more than 22 feet, the jet must also be lowered into the well. Then two pipes lead between pump and jet. One, a pressure pipe, is smaller than the other, a suction pipe. Water is pumped down the pressure pipe, through the jet and upward into the suction pipe. The jetted water draws some well water along with it and up to the intake side of the pump. Excess water is diverted from the pump to the pressure tank. A jet should be located no

Ugly but workable, this set-up gets spring water out of a canyon and 300 feet up to a house. The storage tank (rear) collects the spring's flow. A submersible pump in foreground tank pumps it.

more than 20 feet above the lowest water level in the well. Water delivery of any pump depends on the lift and delivery head or pressure. The higher the head, the fewer gallons per minute delivery. Each person uses about 40 gallons of water a day, but water delivery must be much faster because use is periodic. Minimum pump capacity recommended for a house is 550 gallons per hour.

You can buy submersible or jet pumps and their controls from your dealer and install them yourself. They come with or without pressure tanks and on/off pressure switches.

PE PIPE

If the well is more than about 150 feet deep, it's best to have the installation done by the well-driller. If you do it, use plastic pipe for the down pipe in the well. Size depends on pump capacity. Read the instructions with your pump. Same for wiring it. You can handle about 150 feet of pipe and submersible pump or about 100 feet of double jet pipes without a hoist. In any case, you should provide some means of stopping the pipe's descent into the well so you can make connections or rest. It's a job for two people.

Use a sanitary well seal in the well casing at the upper end to keep out contaminants. The top of the well may be above ground or installed in a well-drained pit. If you prefer, you can bury the well underground and run the water pipes directly into a pressure tank inside the house. For this, use what's called a pitless adapter. Get the parts from your dealer. If you like, you can always rig up a windmill to pump water. But getting all the parts together will take some doing.

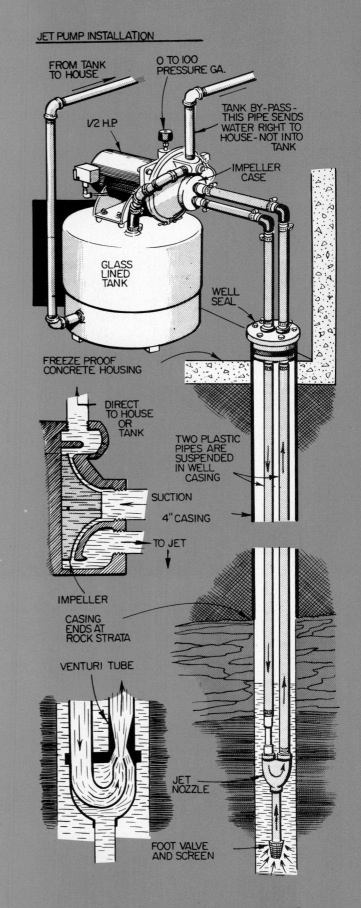

JET PUMP INSTALLATION

FROM TANK TO HOUSE

0 TO 100 PRESSURE GA.

1/2 H.P.

TANK BY-PASS – THIS PIPE SENDS WATER RIGHT TO HOUSE - NOT INTO TANK

IMPELLER CASE

GLASS LINED TANK

WELL SEAL

FREEZE PROOF CONCRETE HOUSING

DIRECT TO HOUSE OR TANK

TWO PLASTIC PIPES ARE SUSPENDED IN WELL CASING

SUCTION

4" CASING

TO JET

IMPELLER

CASING ENDS AT ROCK STRATA

VENTURI TUBE

JET NOZZLE

FOOT VALVE AND SCREEN

CAPTIVE AIR PUMP

AIR CHARGE SEALED INTO TANK - NO VOLUME CONTROL NEEDED

36 GAL.

BAG FULL

VINYL BAG LINER

EMPTY BAG

Install An Underground Sprinkler System

If you don't like hauling hoses around from outlet to outlet, the underground system is for you. You can program the watering at any time of the day; ideal where watering hours are limited.

This elaborate control center requires 115 volts and can be programed to turn eleven separate stations on and off. Smaller 4-head monitors are ideal for smaller homes and cost about $60-$80.

AS YOU PROBABLY know from all those fertilizer and lawn care bills, keeping your land green represents a substantial investment in both time and money. Water has always been a key ingredients to a good lawn, and if Mother Nature can't supply it when needed, you must. This might impose a problem because when you water you must make certain you have the right coverage at just the right time, and you must not just dampen the grass—or drown it.

So it should be done automatically, with you at the helm, and the only way is with an underground sprinkler system that will turn on the right sprinkler head at the right time and water for a predetermined time period. Automatic systems has been around for a long time, being pioneered by the golf courses whose business is keeping grass manicured and by industrial firms and growers who rely on the labor-saving advantages of guaranteeing their landscape-and-crops get that needed moisture.

The home automatic sprinkler system is a new market for the manufacturers of this formerly "industrial" equipment. Built-in automatic systems represent a long lasting home improvement investment. They are trouble free and will really save you time to say nothing of their contribution to a beautiful lawn.

You have seen how they work; underground pipes feed individual sprinkler heads designed to cover a specific area. If you have a ¾" or a 1" water service entrance you could not possibly handle a dozen sprinkler heads so your lawn is divided into sections, and these individual sections are controlled by the monitor. The moni-

This head can be adjusted to cover all or part of an 80' (or less) circle. The number of heads in any one line depends upon the water pressure and pipe size. Minimum pressure is 40 pounds.

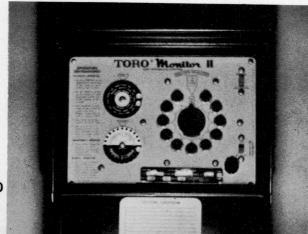

Have a better lawn with less work by predetermining how much and when you need water. Then let this automatic unit carry out your instructions.

tor, being electrically operated, merely opens and controls the valve for each section at any time you wish and for a period of up to one hour. Of course, the cycle can be repeated after all sections have been watered.

Economical plastic pipe (polyethylene and PVC) is installed about 6" below the ground and feeds individual sprinkler heads. All the section lines return to a manifold, which is equipped with a hydraulic or electric valves that are opened and closed by a signal from the monitor. It's as simple as that!

Cost is difficult to figure since all installations are not the same, but as a rule of thumb you can plan to spend anywhere from 10 to 15 cents per square foot of lawn area for a complete system. This includes all pipe, the heads, fittings, the important control valves and the brain—the monitor.

Our recommendation is simple: you can easily do the work but have the system laid out by your dealer who can specify the exact heads you need for any area, choose the correct number of valves and also select the monitor. After all, if your lawn requires only four stations, you need not spend the added money for an 11-station monitor. And don't think you must dig up your lawn either. Small trenchers are available that cut a slot about an inch wide, which is usually covered in a few weeks with new grass. Or you can make a V-slot with a spade, tuck the pipe in the bottom of the V and then force the soil back. The scar disappears promptly—especially since you now *cannot* neglect your watering responsibility!

Many types of heads are available, and all can be adjusted for diameter and part-of-circle coverage. This pop-up unit produces a mist and was designed for small areas. Many run off one line.

This manifold has three 24-volt electric valves. All sprinkler systems should be equipped with a vacuum breaker, the large fitting above the pipe leading to the inside. Build a box around valves.

Nothing fancy to these branches because they are covered up. The toughest part of any system is digging the trenches to accommodate the pipe. Seek dealer's advice as to pipe sizes, pressures.

121

Plumbing Emergencies

A sudden leak, or a clog you can't fix can be both unhealthy and damaging. Here are some pointers we learned the hard way.

SOONER OR LATER one of many plumbing emergencies may come to your house. No need to fear. Knowing what to do and being programmed to do it in a hurry beats all hair-tearing. Look over the various plumbing problems and be ready when they come. Know where your tools are. Know where the water-supply system's valves are. See that everyone does. Then you can be ready to save your house from possible damage, plus saving a good deal of money in avoiding a call for professional help.

The most valuable thing you can do in a real plumbing emergency is to keep a cool head. When water is running out on an upstairs floor, dripping from the downstairs ceilings onto your finest furniture and pouring from ceiling electrical fixtures, it isn't easy to stay calm. You can just picture the damage that is being done above ceilings and behind walls, let alone to your furnishings. It's tough to say whether to move the furniture out of the way first or run and turn off the house main shutoff valve first. If you move the furniture, at least it will suffer no further damage, but the water is still running and doing its worst to ruin your house. At any rate, as quickly as you can, get to that shutoff valve and stop the flow of additional water.

MOP UP

Then you have time, time to forget about the plumbing for a while and minimize water damage to your house. Mop up water on wood floors. If water has run into any electrical fixture boxes, turn off the power at least to them, perhaps to the whole house. This will forestall short-circuits until things can dry up a bit.

Wetted walls and ceilings should be left alone. If you fuss with them while they're wet,

you can easily punch through. Then the wall will have to be replastered or new plasterboard installed. Better to leave them alone, letting them dry out naturally. When they dry, their original stiffness will come back. Perhaps, then, the stains can be painted over without having to replace the material. If not, you can always do it later.

WHERE'S THE LEAK

Meanwhile, back at the plumbing, you must find and fix the problem before your house can have water again. If it's a stopped-up drain, see the chapter on unclogging. If water running into a clogged fixture drain is turned off, it should be safe to turn on the main shutoff valve and restore water service to the rest of the house. This takes you out of the hot-seat. Takes it out of the emergency category, you might say.

But if the problem is a leak, you don't get off that easily. Leaks can be tough to find and fix. If it is out in the open—say at a fixture's supply pipe—you are in luck. Replacing the fitting or the whole supply pipe will restore the plumbing to normal.

A behind-the-wall leak, or one inaccessible behind the ceiling or floor is much more troublesome. Your task is to positively identify it before you tear out any wall, floor or ceiling materials. Otherwise, you'll be like a dog digging out a gopher—a hole here and a hole there, all to be repaired later, and still no gopher.

LISTENING FOR IT

Think about it for a moment. Where was water coming out? What was the highest point you saw evidences of it? Start from there and work up. Get someone to help you. While you listen at the point of suspicion, have them turn the water back on. Can water be heard spurting or dripping? Turn off and move to a new position. Try again. Closer this time?

The most common leak spots are, as you might think, at joints. Others are along outside walls in winter when water in the pipes can freeze, then thaw and leak out. If the temperature has been very cold, a freeze-up leak is probably it. In a sweat-soldered copper or plastic system that has been water-hammering, leaks may come at right-angle turns where a fitting has been split off by overpressures.

Another fine way of pinning down leaking is to eliminate the hot-water supply system. Do this by turning off the inlet valve to the water heater, then having your helper open the main shutoff valve. If leaking still occurs, it isn't from the hot-water system. Thus you can look on the right side of fixtures, instead of on the left side. That makes for smaller holes.

If there are other water-supply system shutoff valves, make use of them in deducing where the leak can be. Sometimes these valves are located in the basement or crawlspace. Turn them off one by one until the leak stops. The last one you turned off controls the pipes containing the leak. Concentrate on them.

OPEN THE WALL

Only when you've pinned down the leak is it time to remove wall, floor or ceiling materials to get at it. Work through as small an opening as possible to minimize patching. Use a drill, keyhole saw, saber saw or whatever's available, even a chisel, to cut through room materials and get at the piping behind them. Be careful not to cut into the pipes themselves, or into electrical wiring hidden in the framing. If you encounter any resistance behind the wall, leave it alone. It's probably a pipe or a wire.

When at last you've exposed the leak, what it is will determine what's to be done. Pipes and fittings can be patched temporarily as described in the chapter on patching. However, in no case should any of these patches be installed behind a wall and then finished over. They must be exposed, accessible, for they're not permanent. Eventually, they'll leak again.

In hidden spots you must make permanent repairs. This means replacing leaky fittings, installing new pipes in place of cracked or leaking ones. The individual chapters on working with various pipe types will give clues as to what method of attack you should use. Damaged portions of pipe and fittings can be cut out and new pipes and fittings made up to replace them. With threaded pipes you'll need to install one union to let the threads all be screwed back together.

If you wish, a temporary patch can be installed and water service restored while you work out a lasting repair. If freezing was the cause of the problem, take steps to see that it doesn't happen again. These are easy while the wall is open. Tuck additional building insulation around the pipe. If the pipe is one that freezes often, wrap it with electrical heating cable and plug that in whenever freeze-proofing is needed. Or you can install PE pipe (in cold-water runs only), which is somewhat proof against freeze damage. You may decide somewhere along the line to call in a professional. If you get at a loss as to what to do, this is your best move.

A plumber, if you've ever called one, seems to charge more than a doctor for his services. Though the actual charge is some $12 to $15 an hour per man, it adds up rapidly because most come with a truck full of tools and a helper. Moreover, if you call him after 5 p.m. or on Saturday or Sunday, you'll probably have to pay double those rates.

ASK A FRIEND

The best way to choose a plumber is by experience—but how do you get experience? If you haven't had much experience with plumbers, ask your neighbors if they have. See if they will recommend one, now, before you need him. In general, a plumber near your home may be your best bet, all other factors equal. He can get there with the least travel time. And travel time is dead time.

Finally, before your plumbing emergency arises, call around and find out what the local plumbers charge. Settle on your man and write his name and telephone number in the emergency section of your phone directory. Then, if he and his work satisfy, stick with him. He should do even better the next time because he'll know you.

A good bet, if your emergency happens during extra-time hours, is to have minimum repairs done then. Enough to protect you and the house. Then see if the plumber will come back during regular hours to complete the job. Or complete it yourself, if you can.

It pays to be able to handle emergencies yourself. That's the purpose of this book. But just don't delay calling in a professional when you need one.